ANIMAL MANDALAS
Adult coloring book

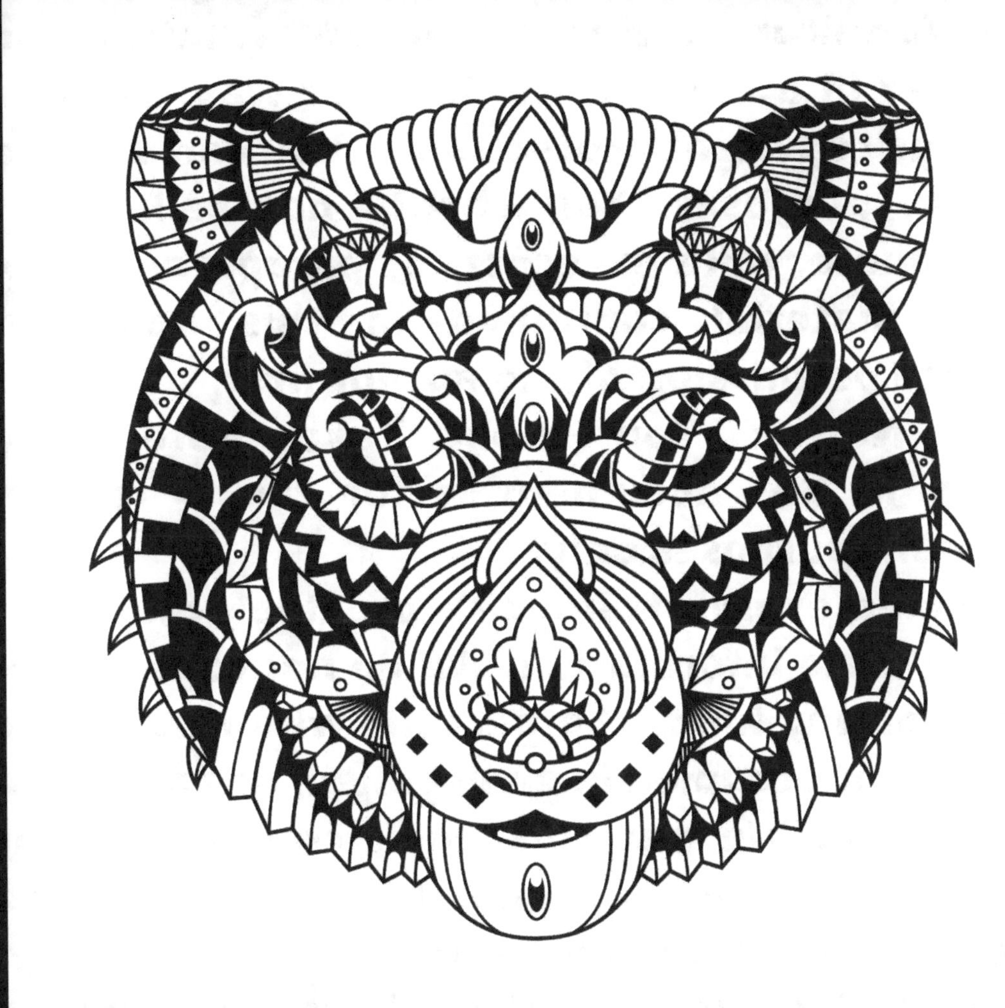

- Christopher Morrison -

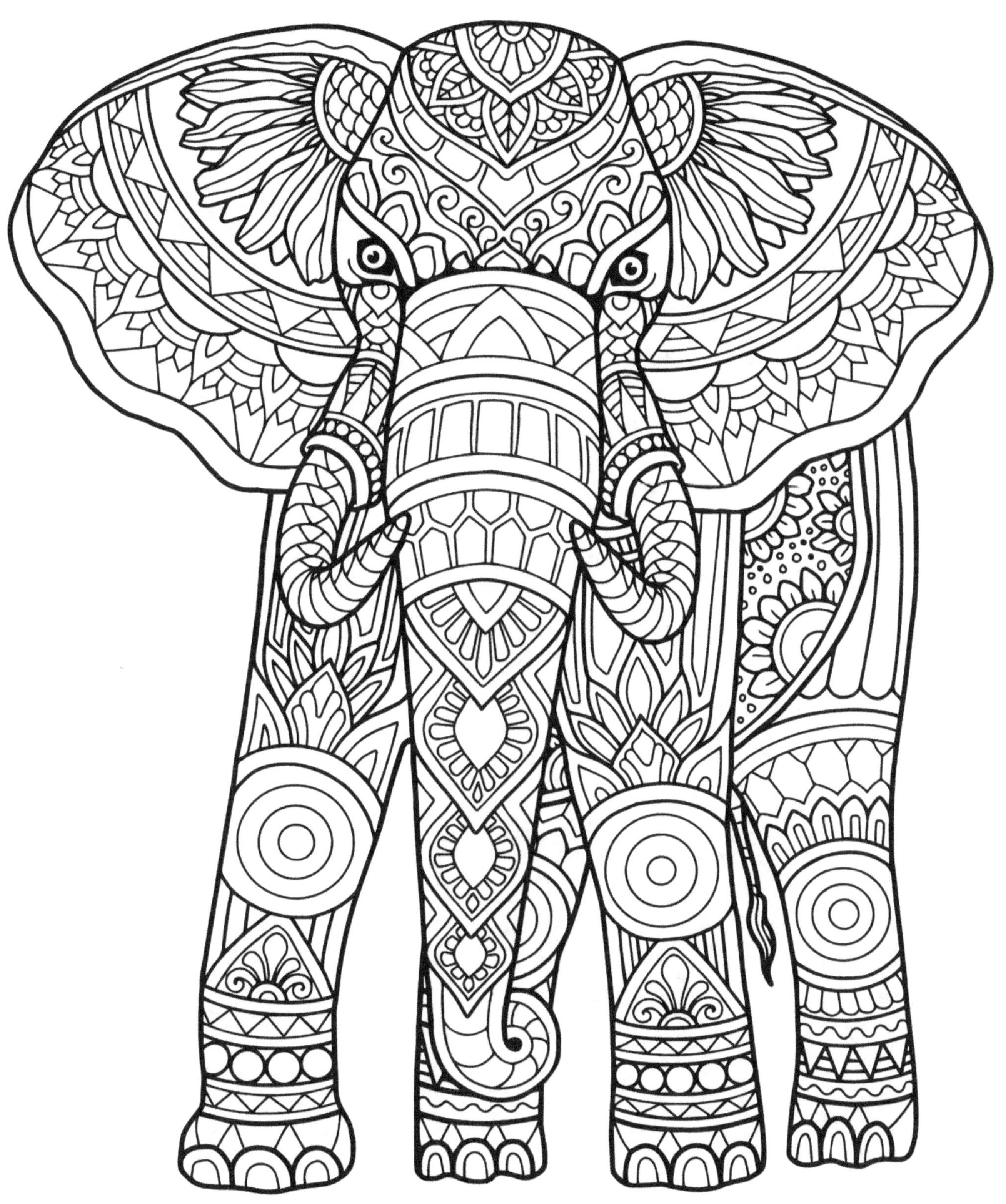

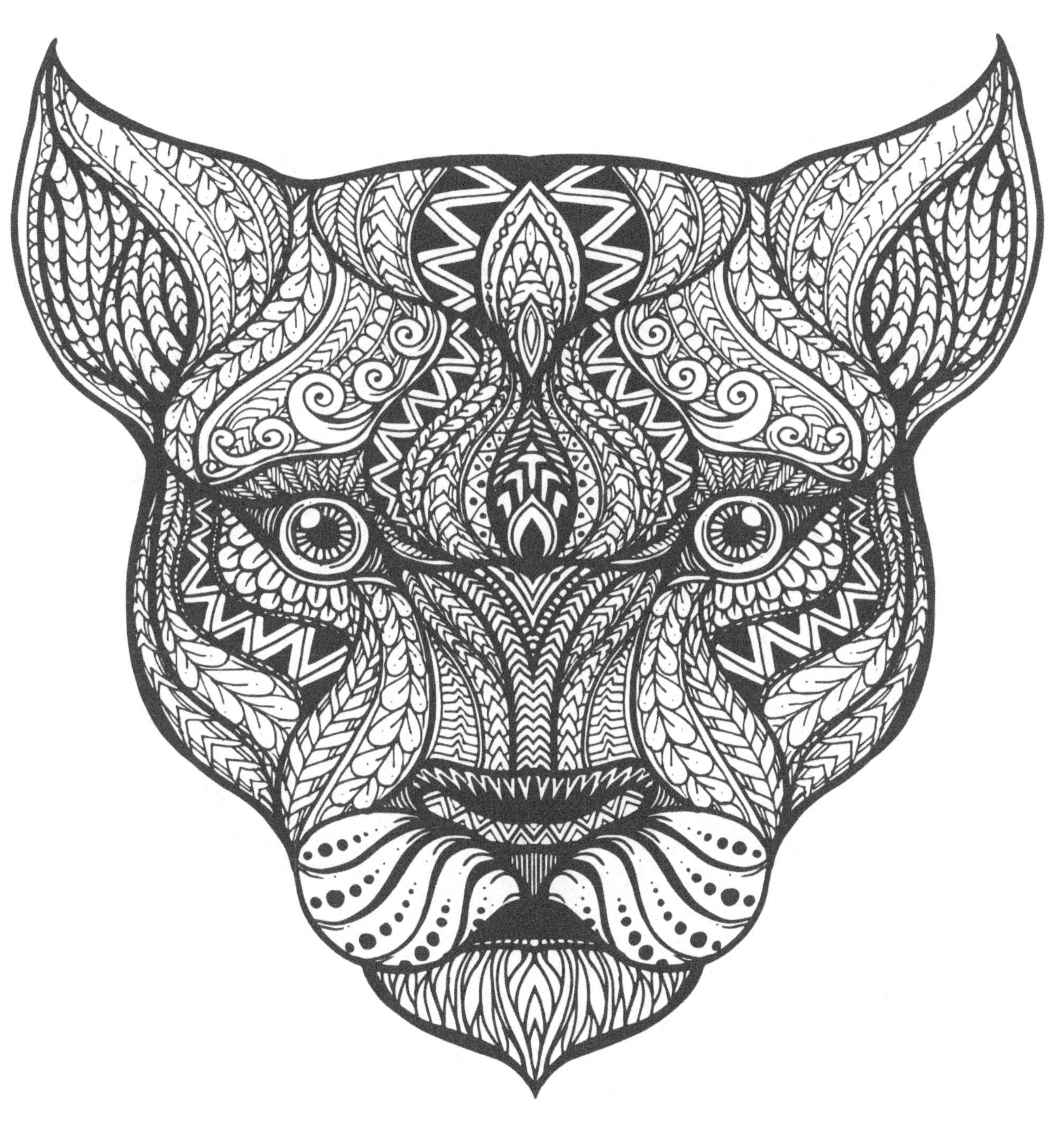

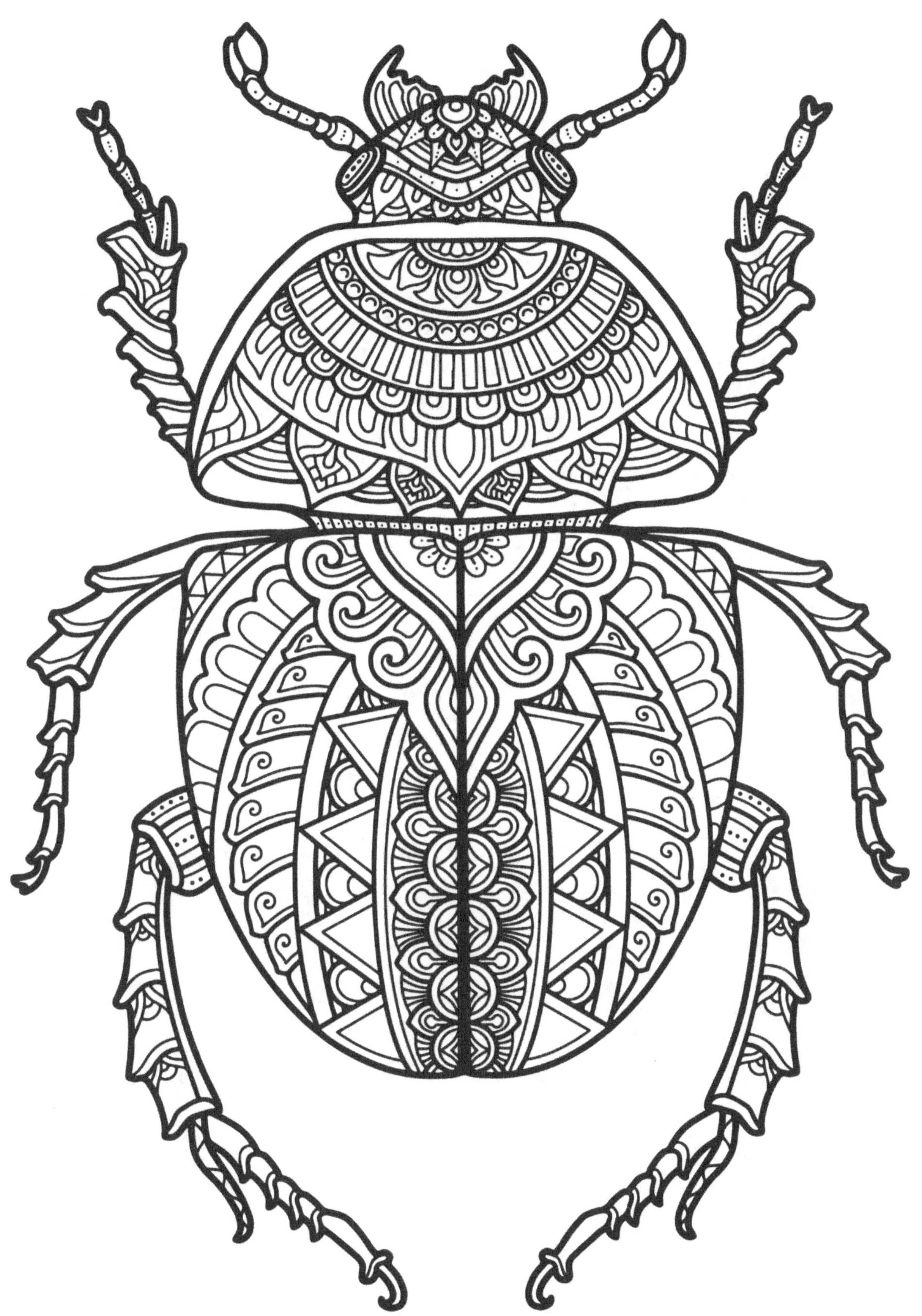

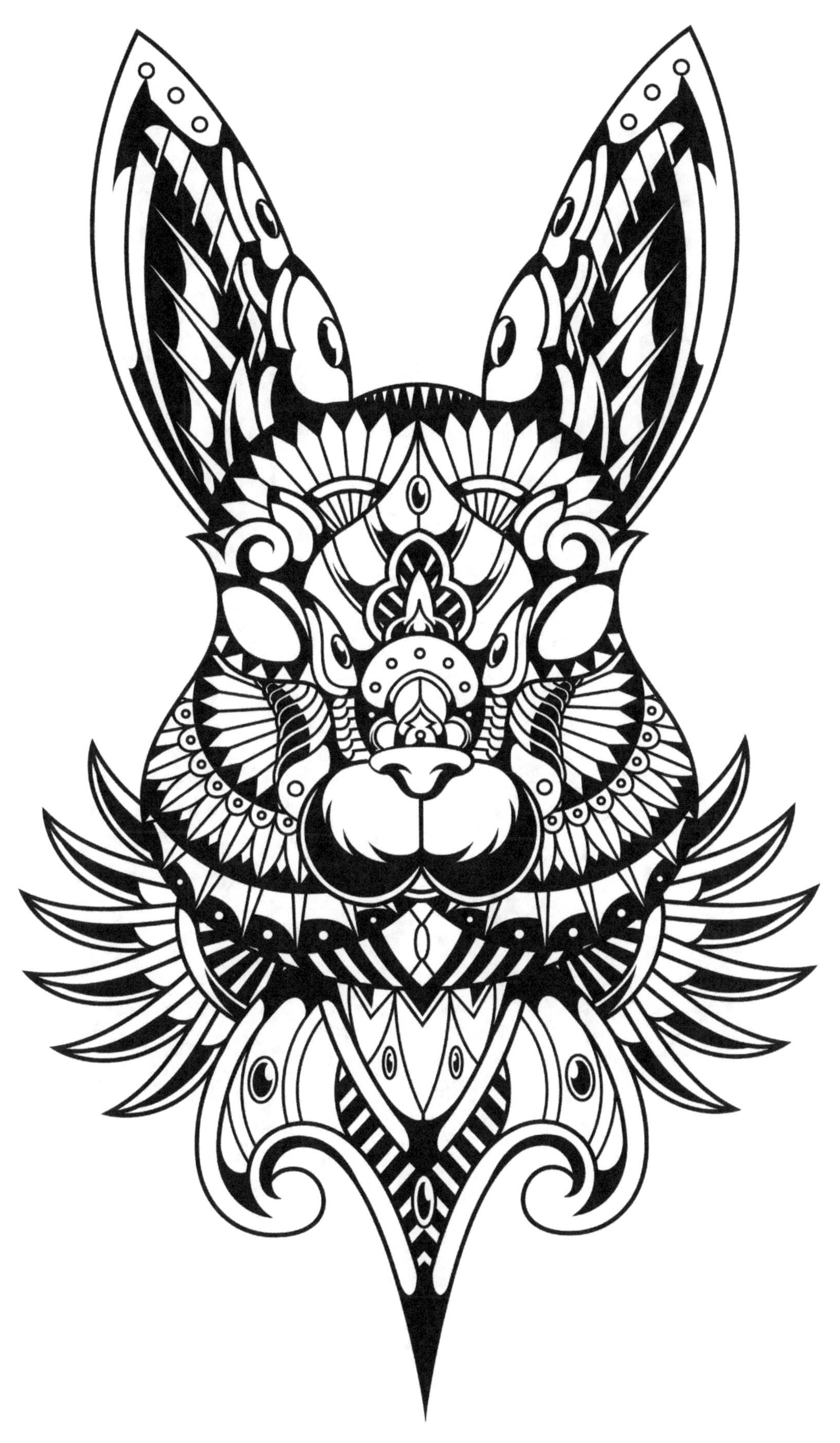

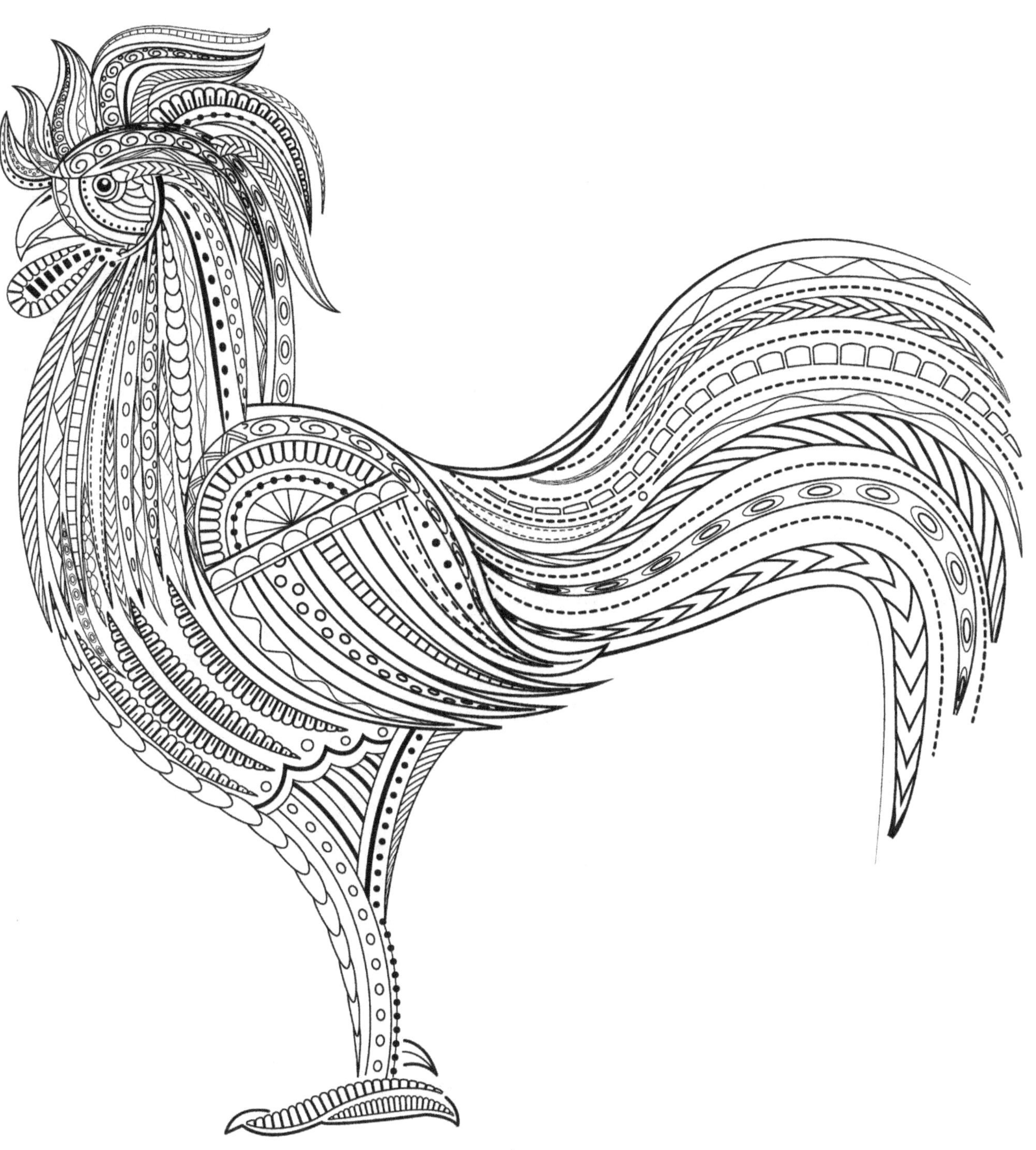

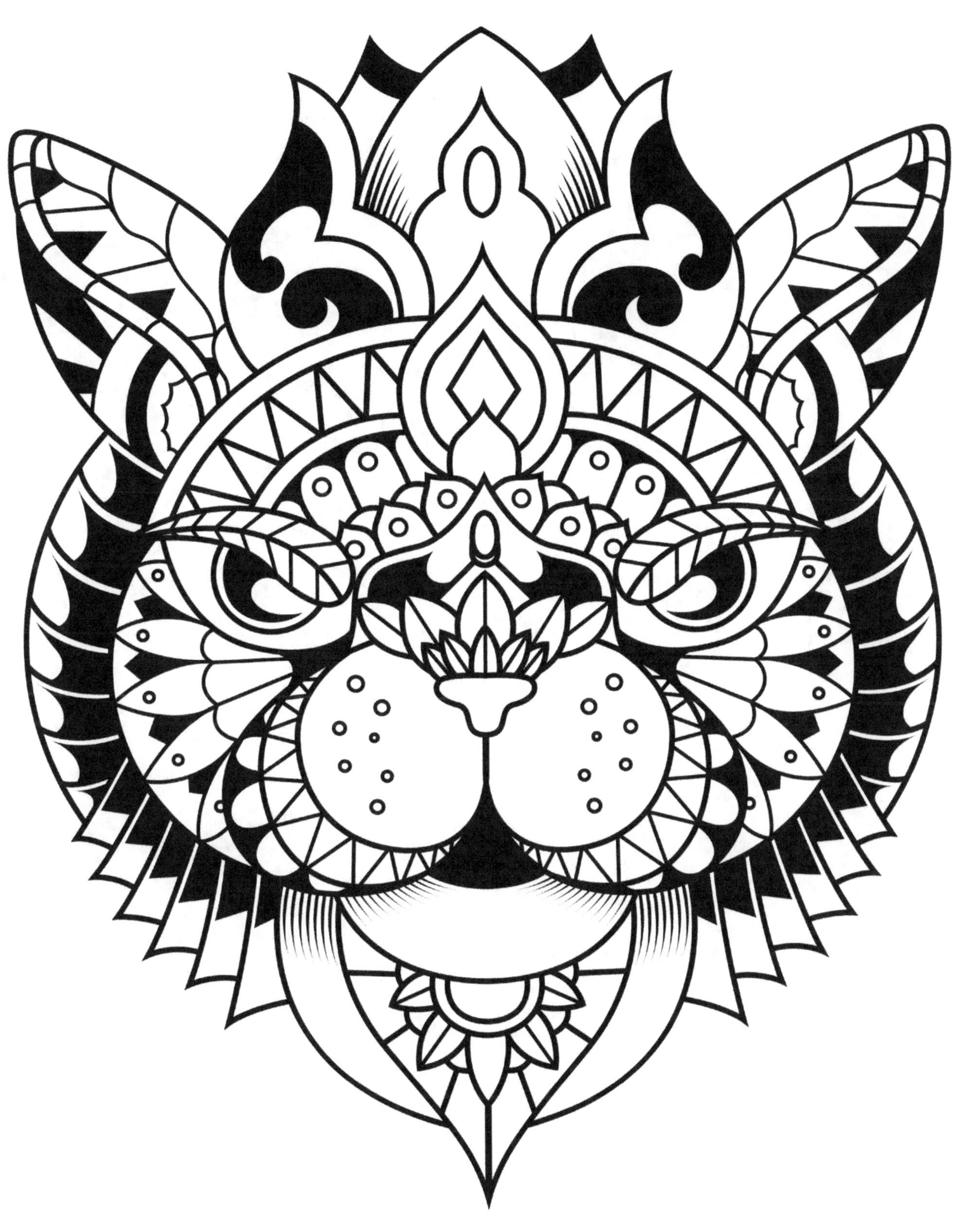

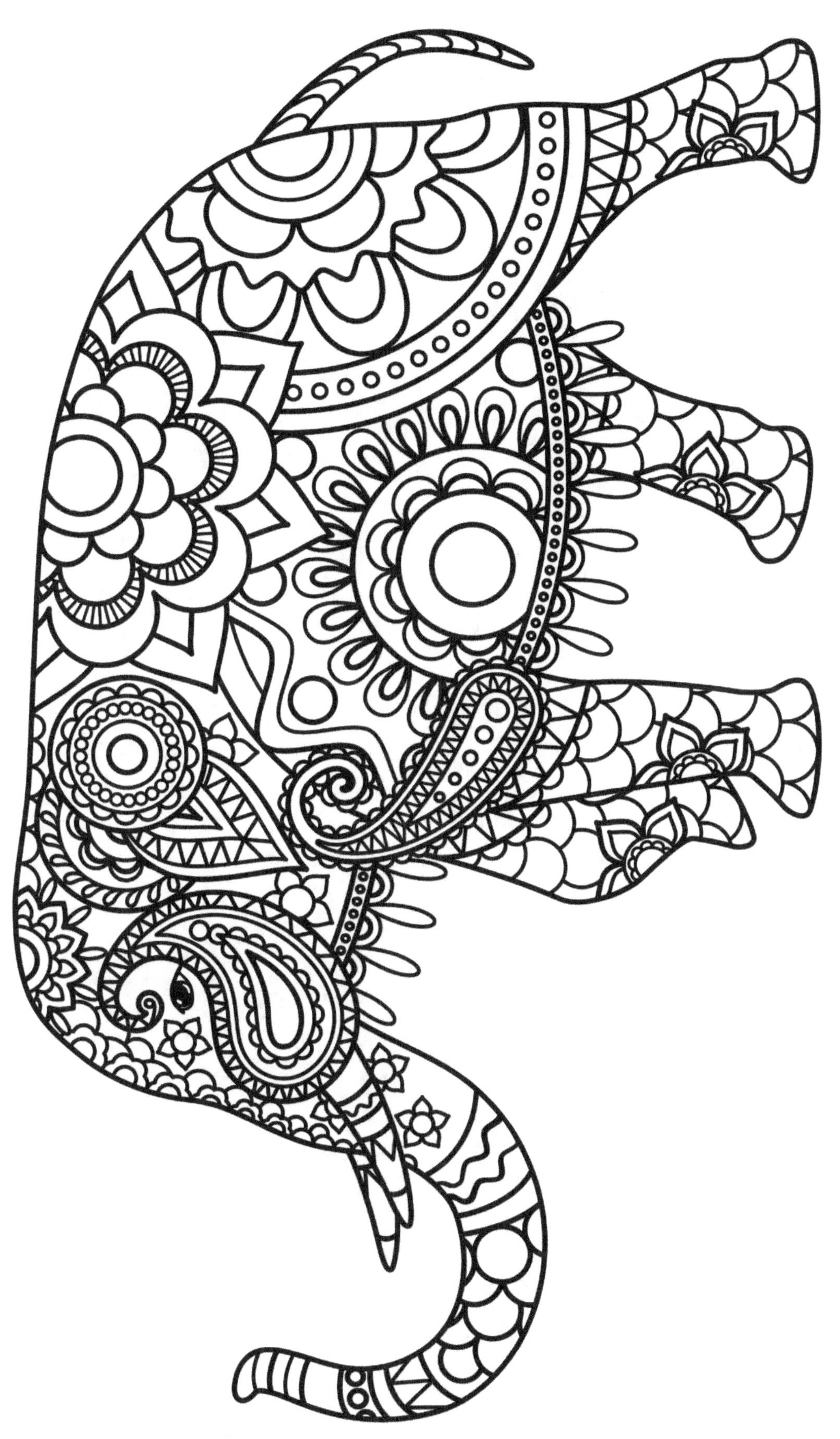

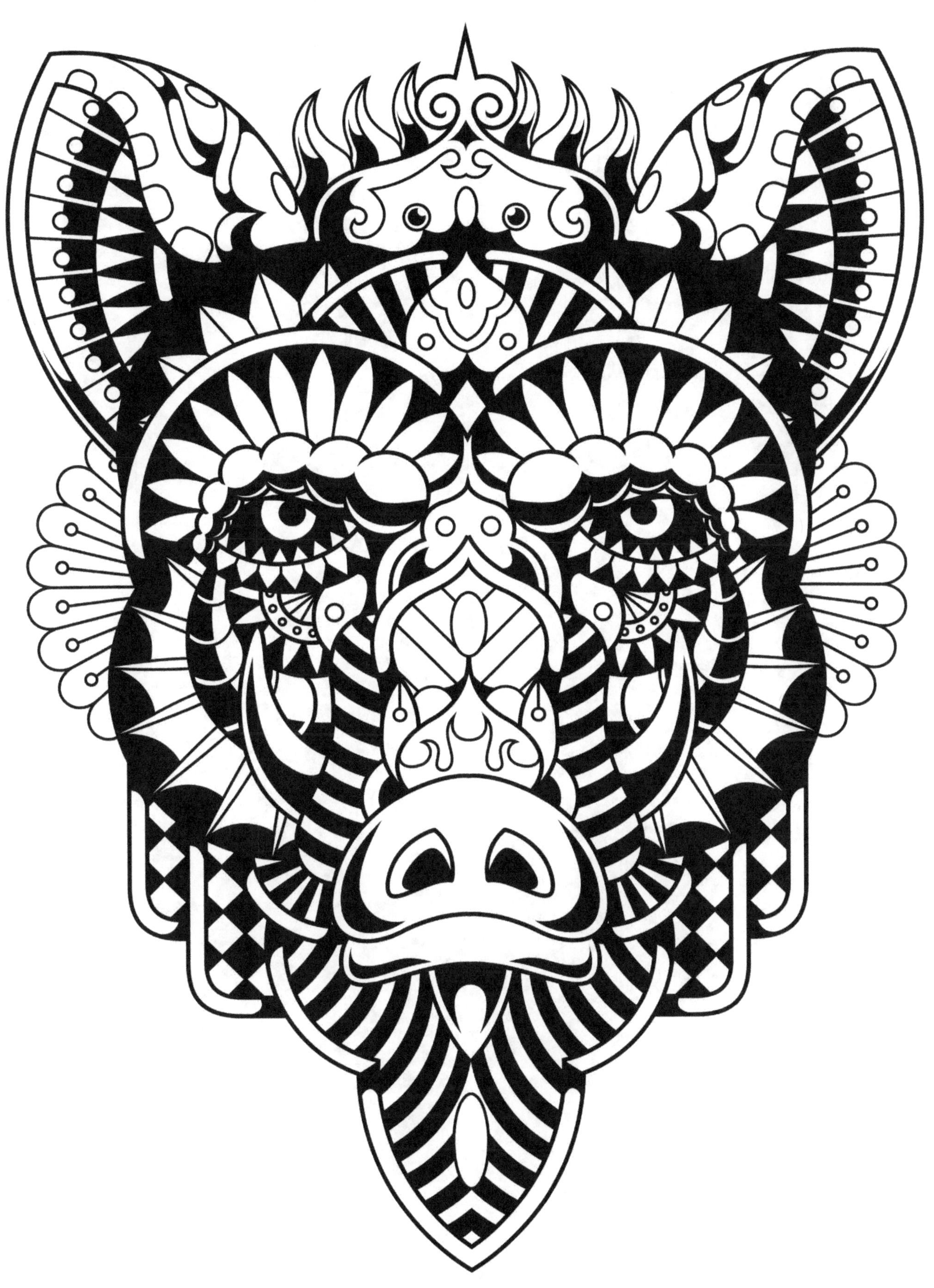

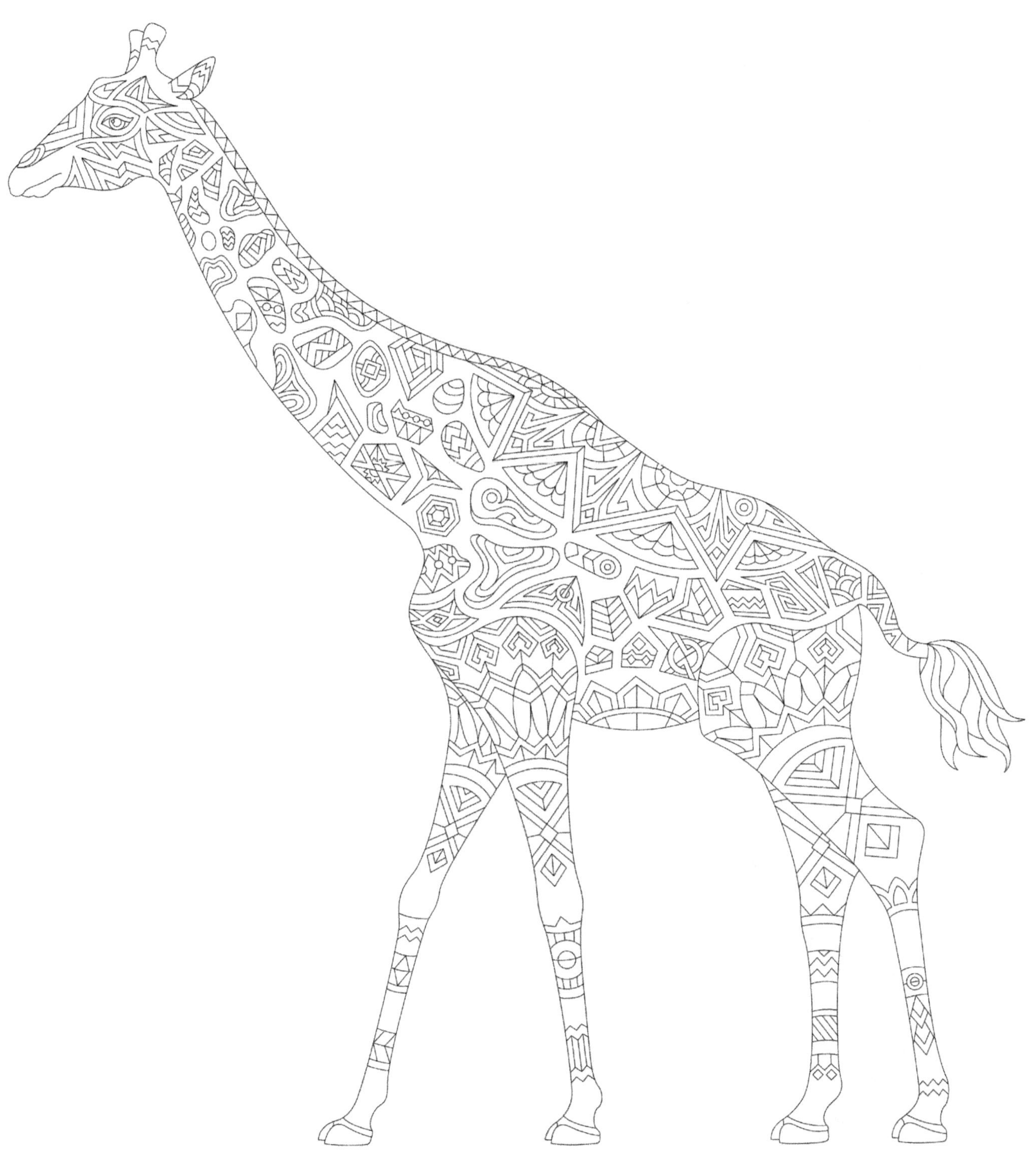

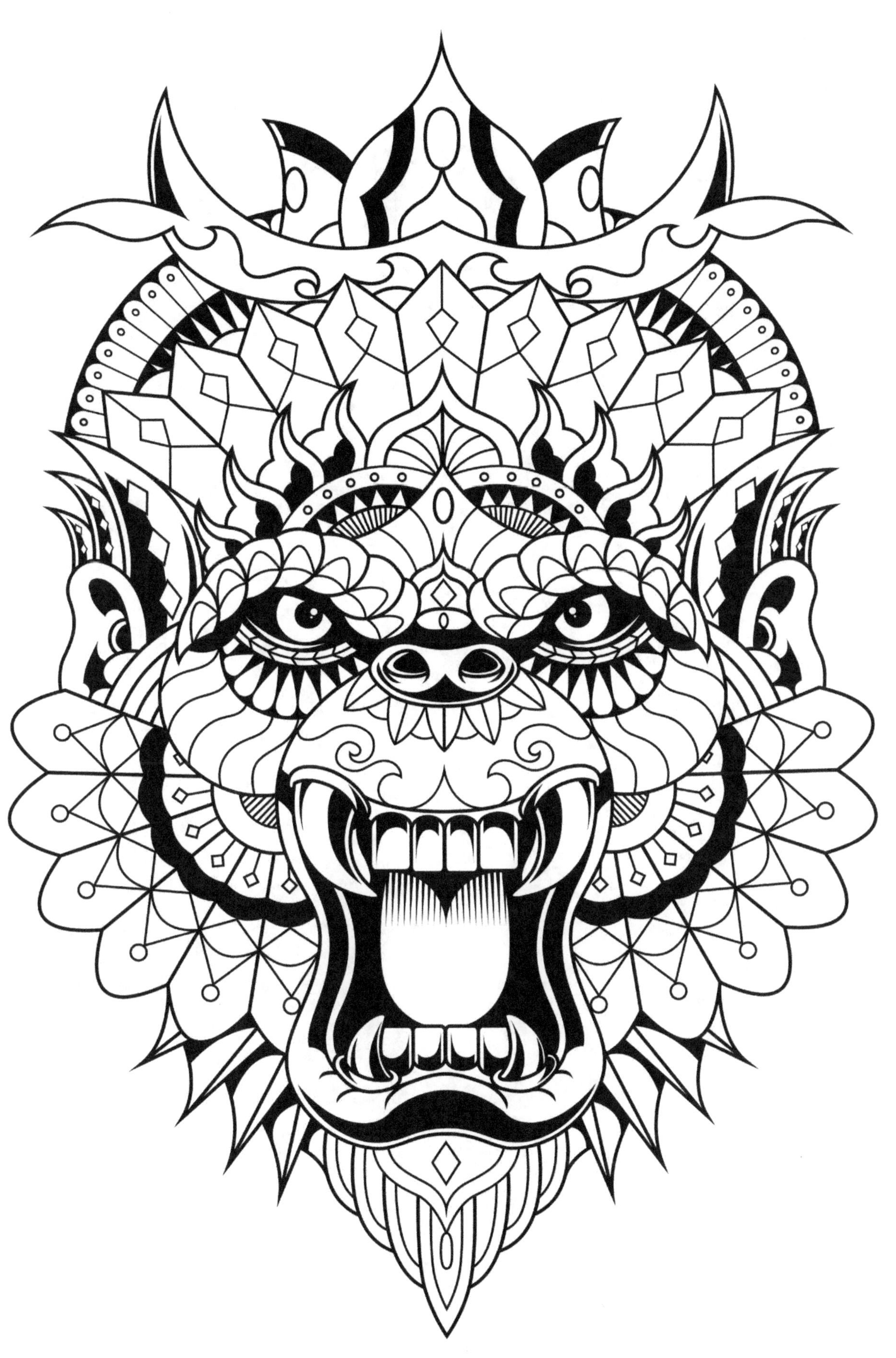

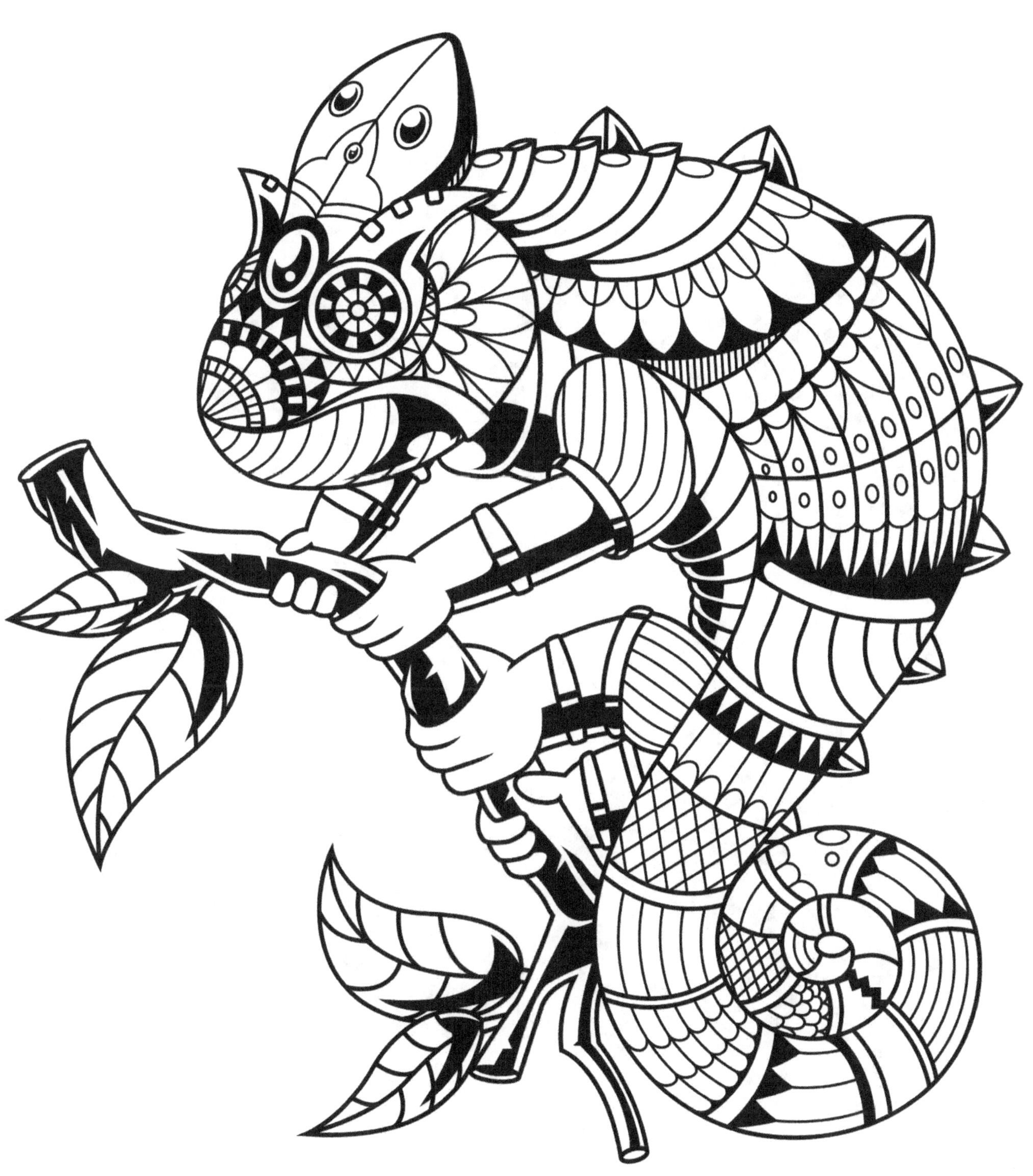

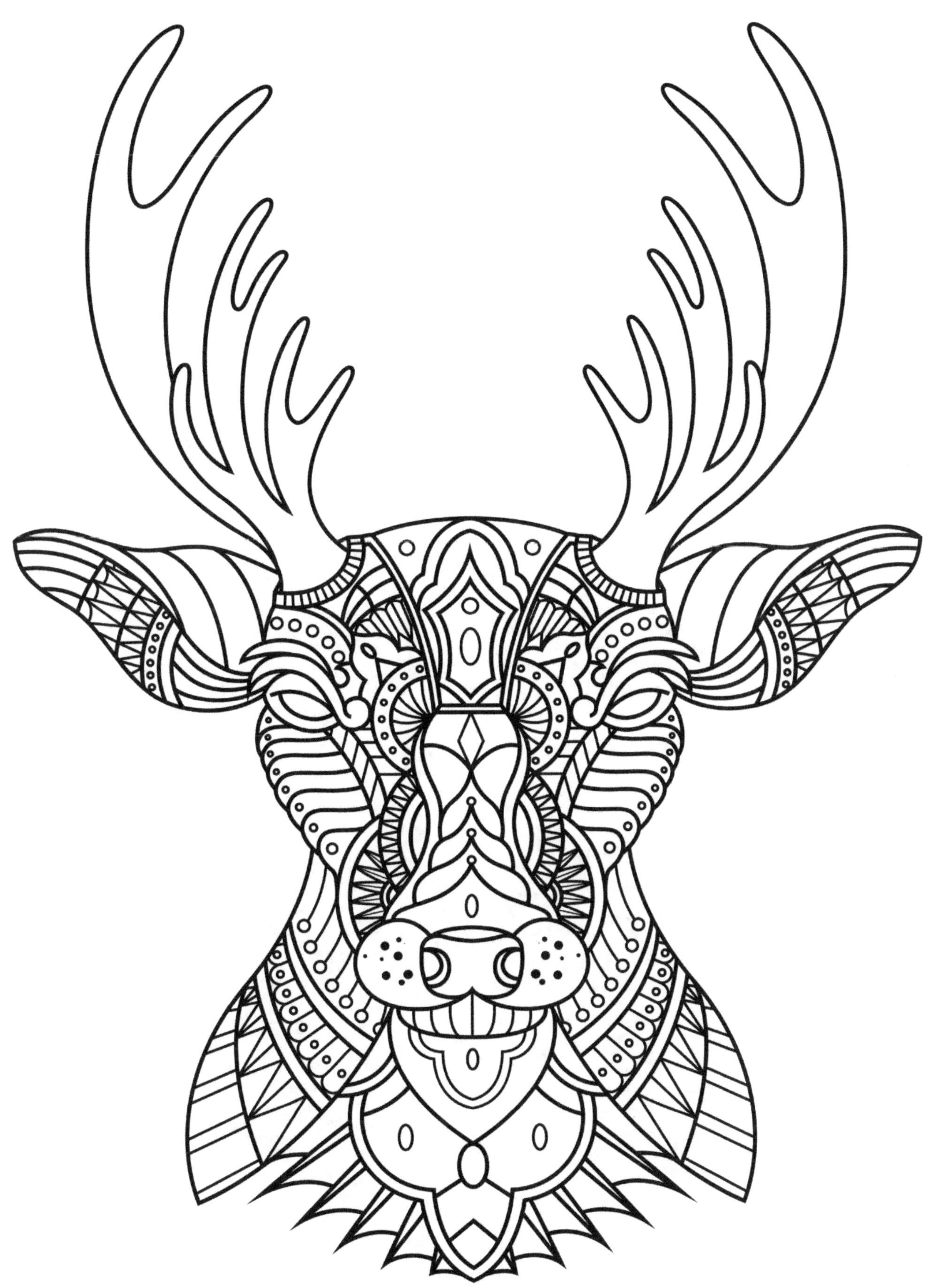

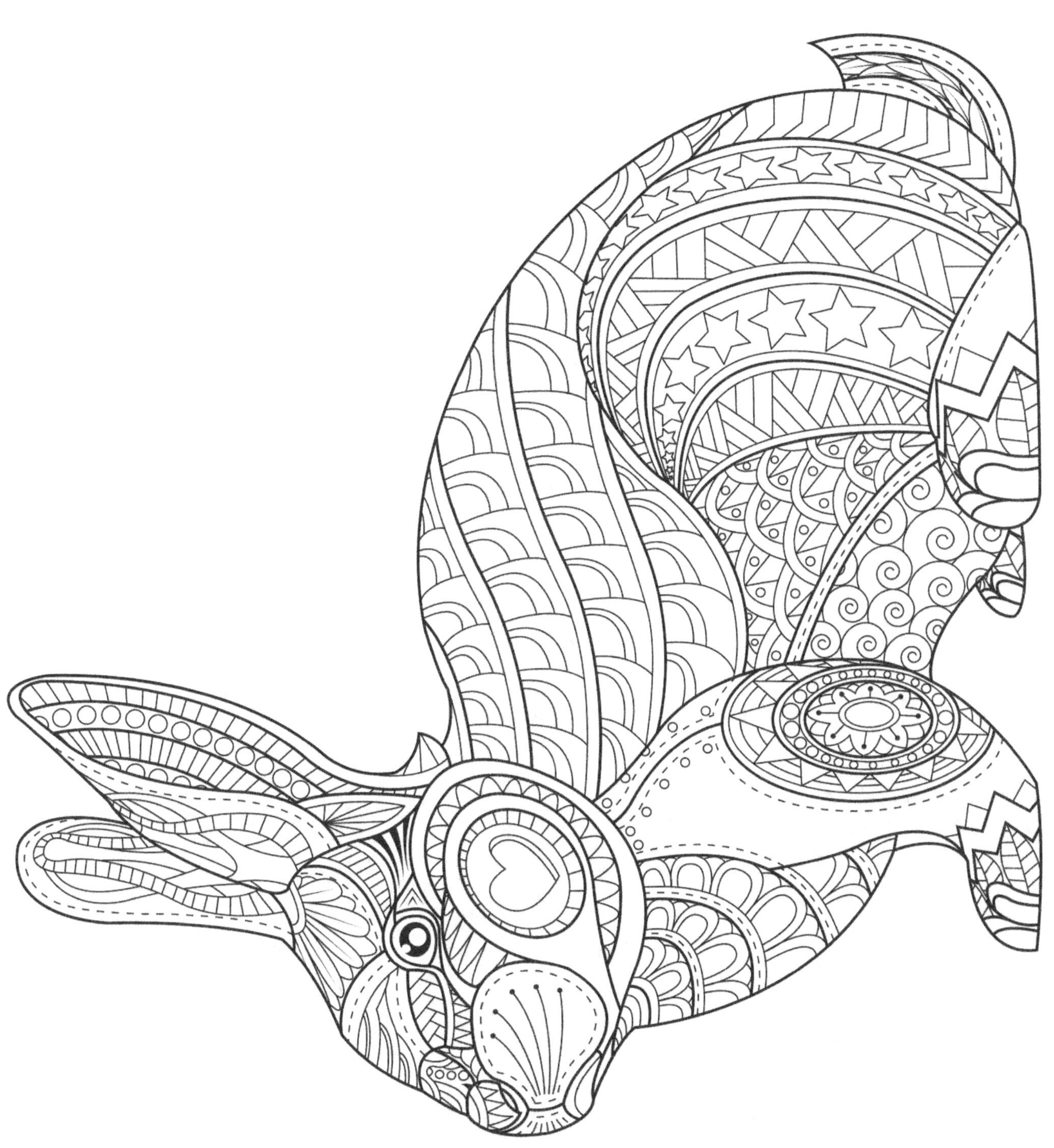

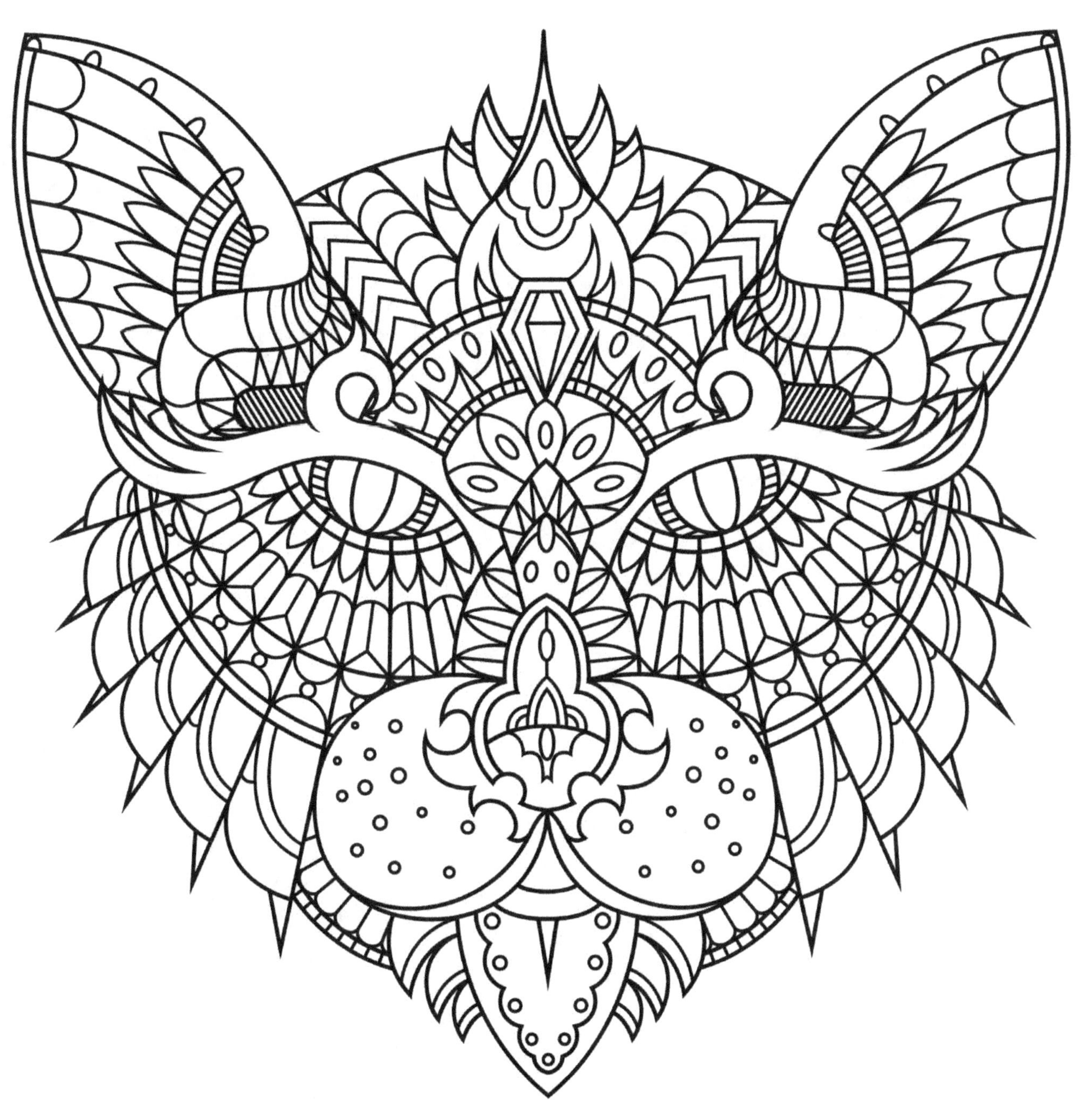

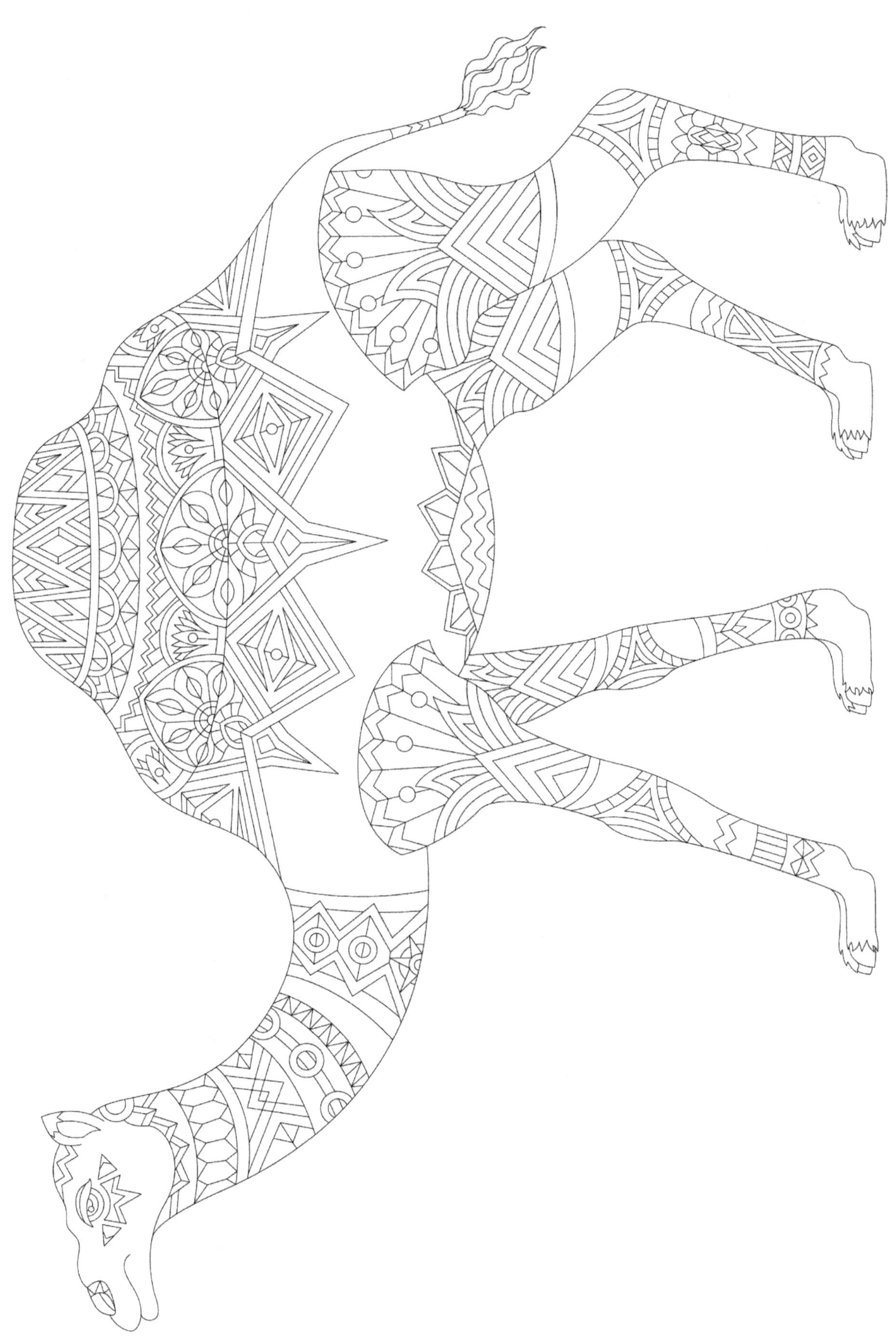

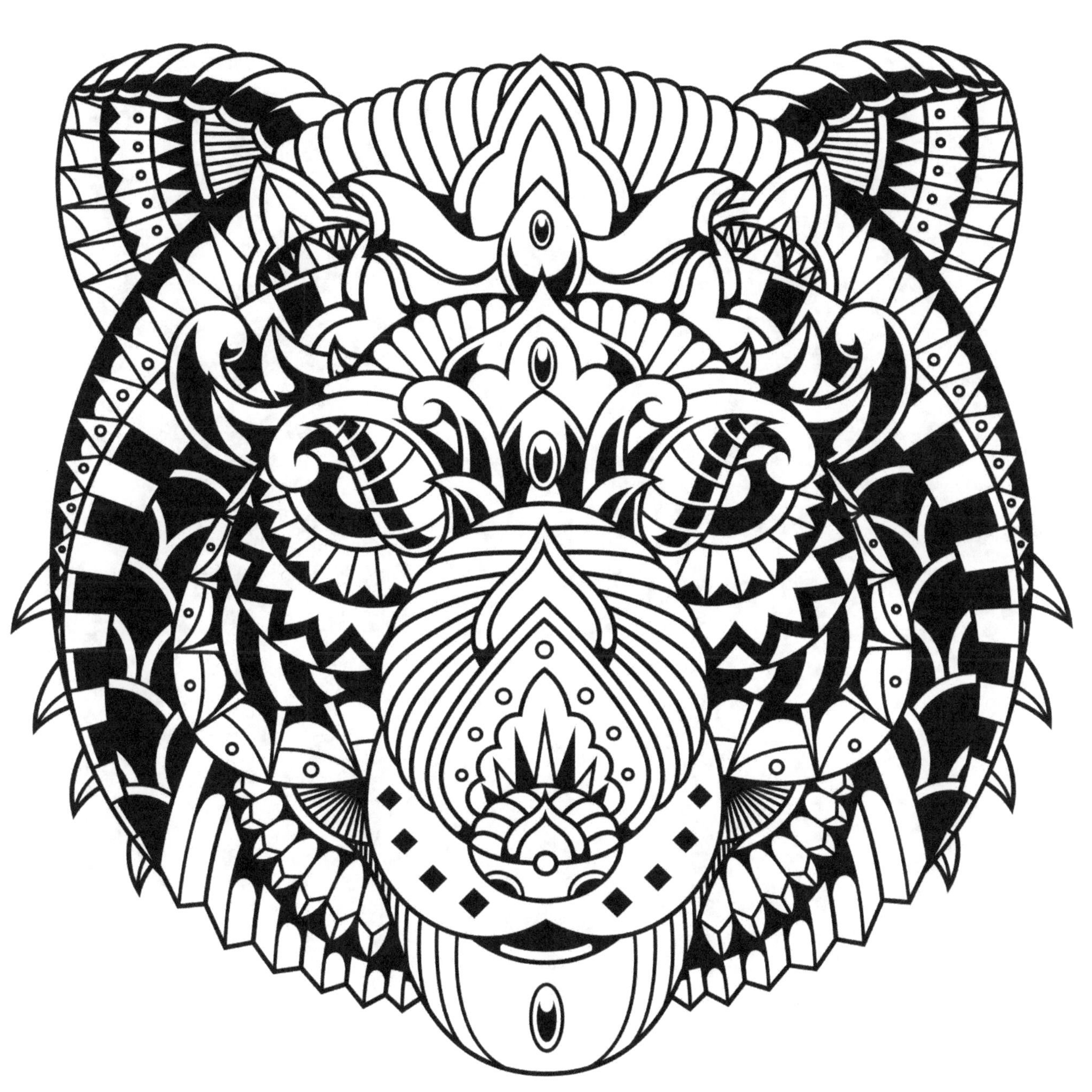

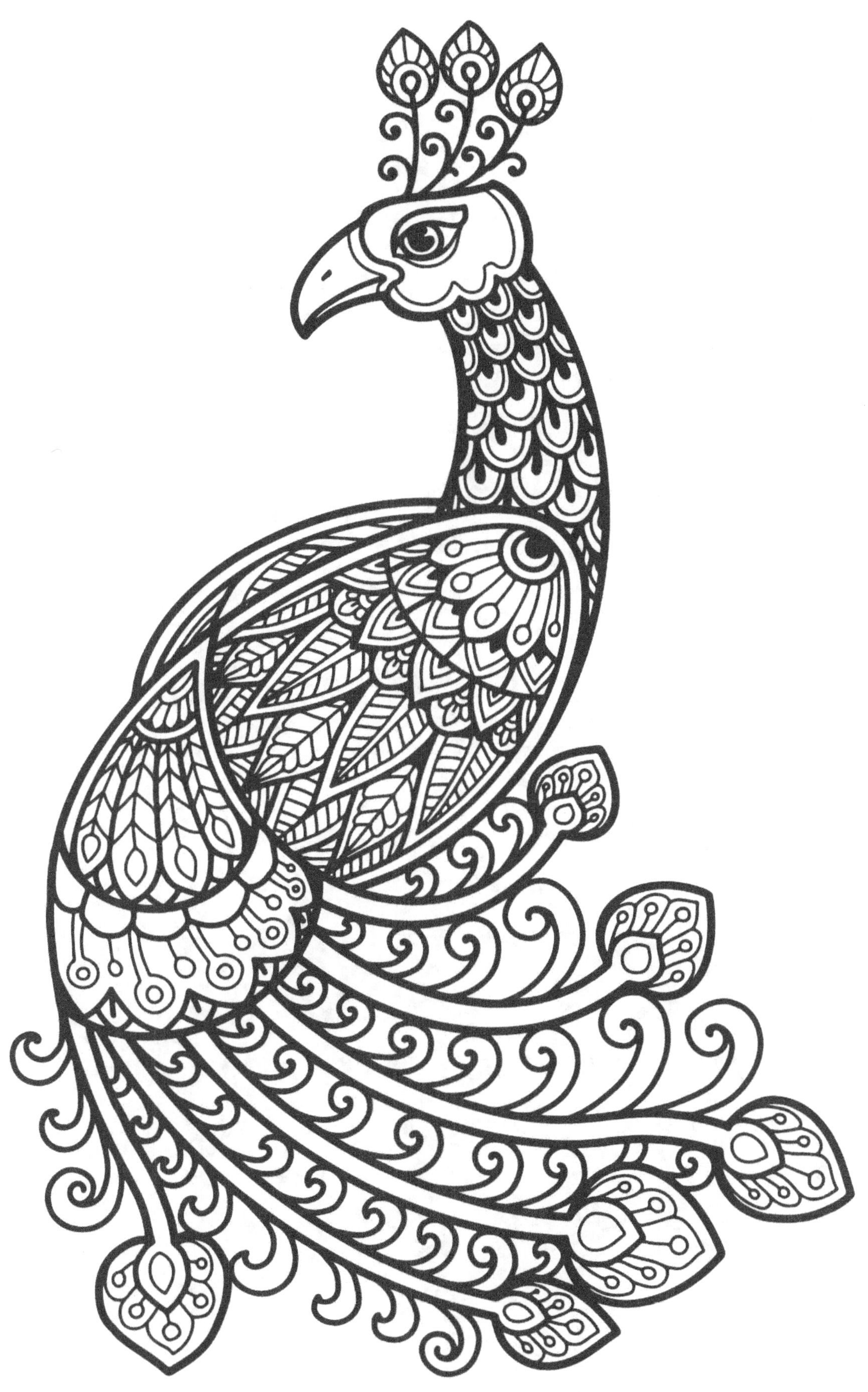

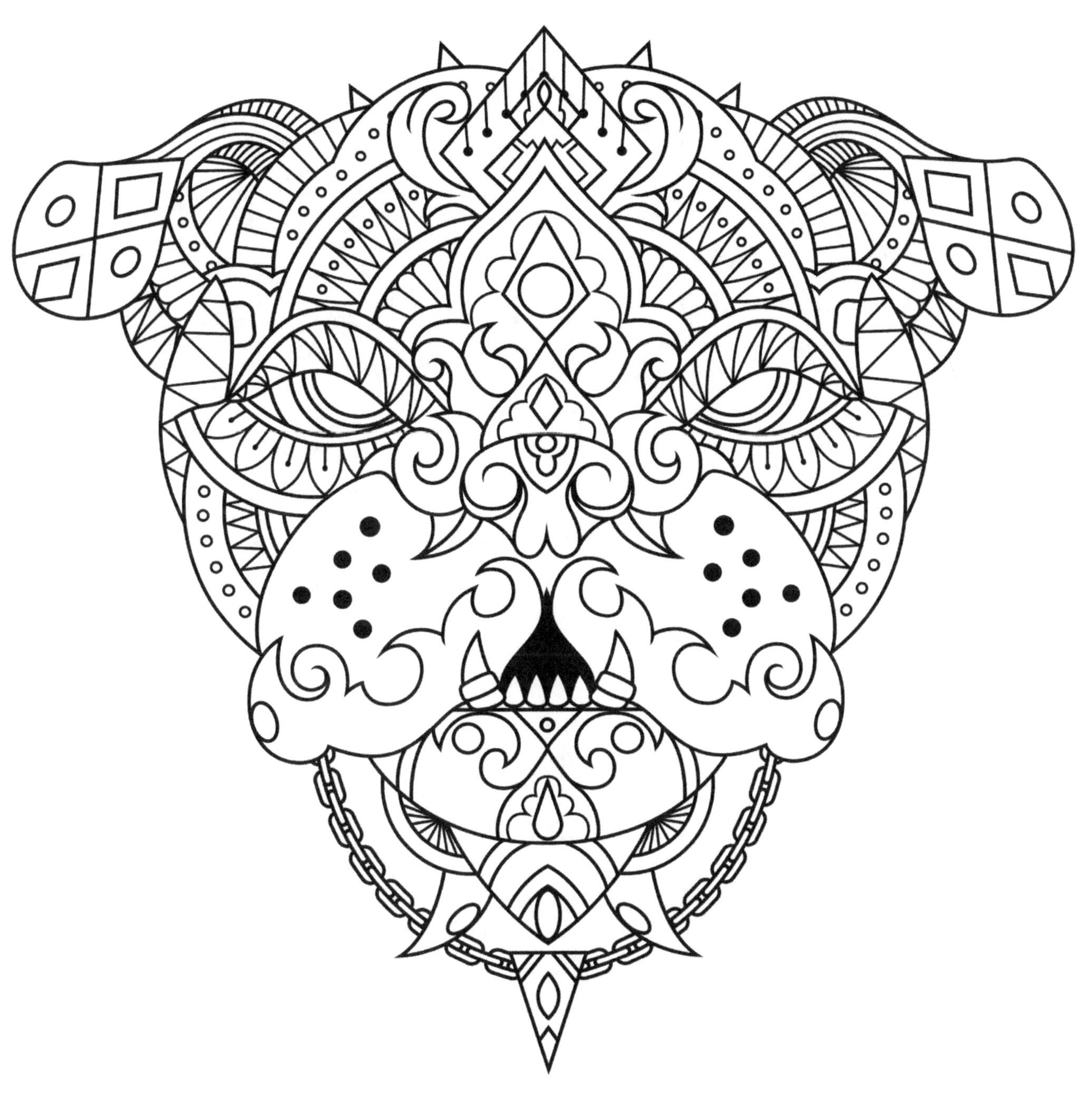

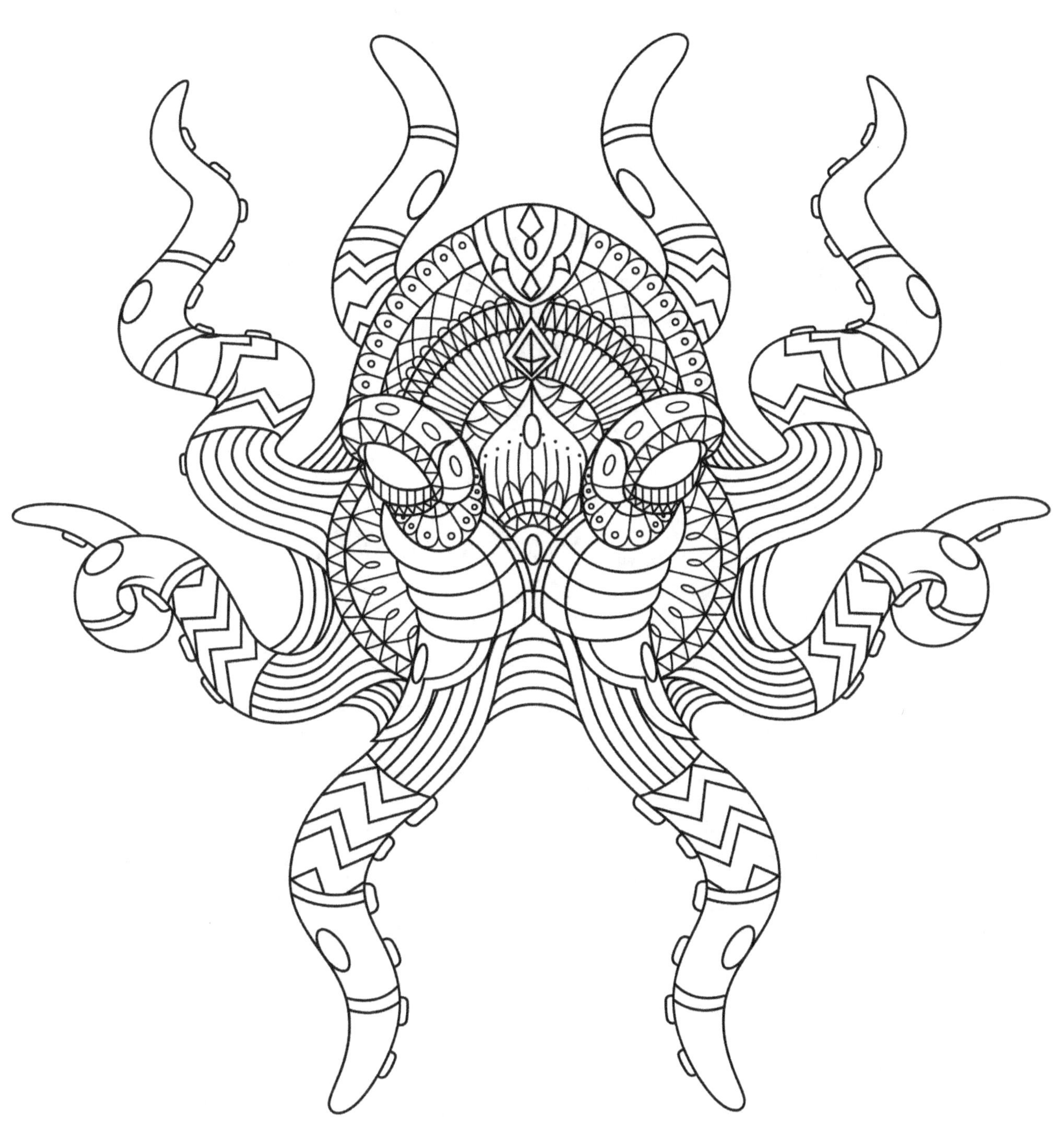

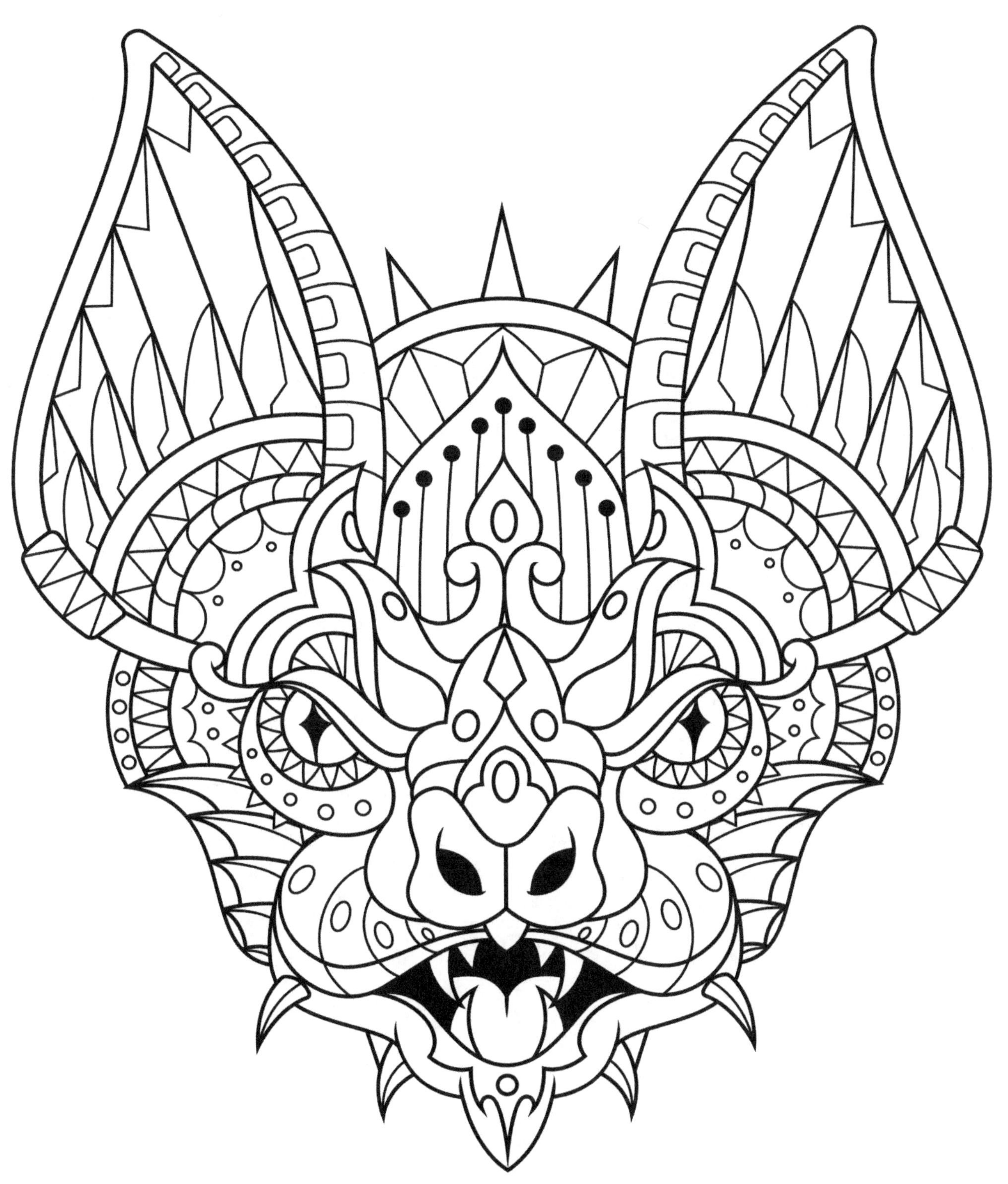

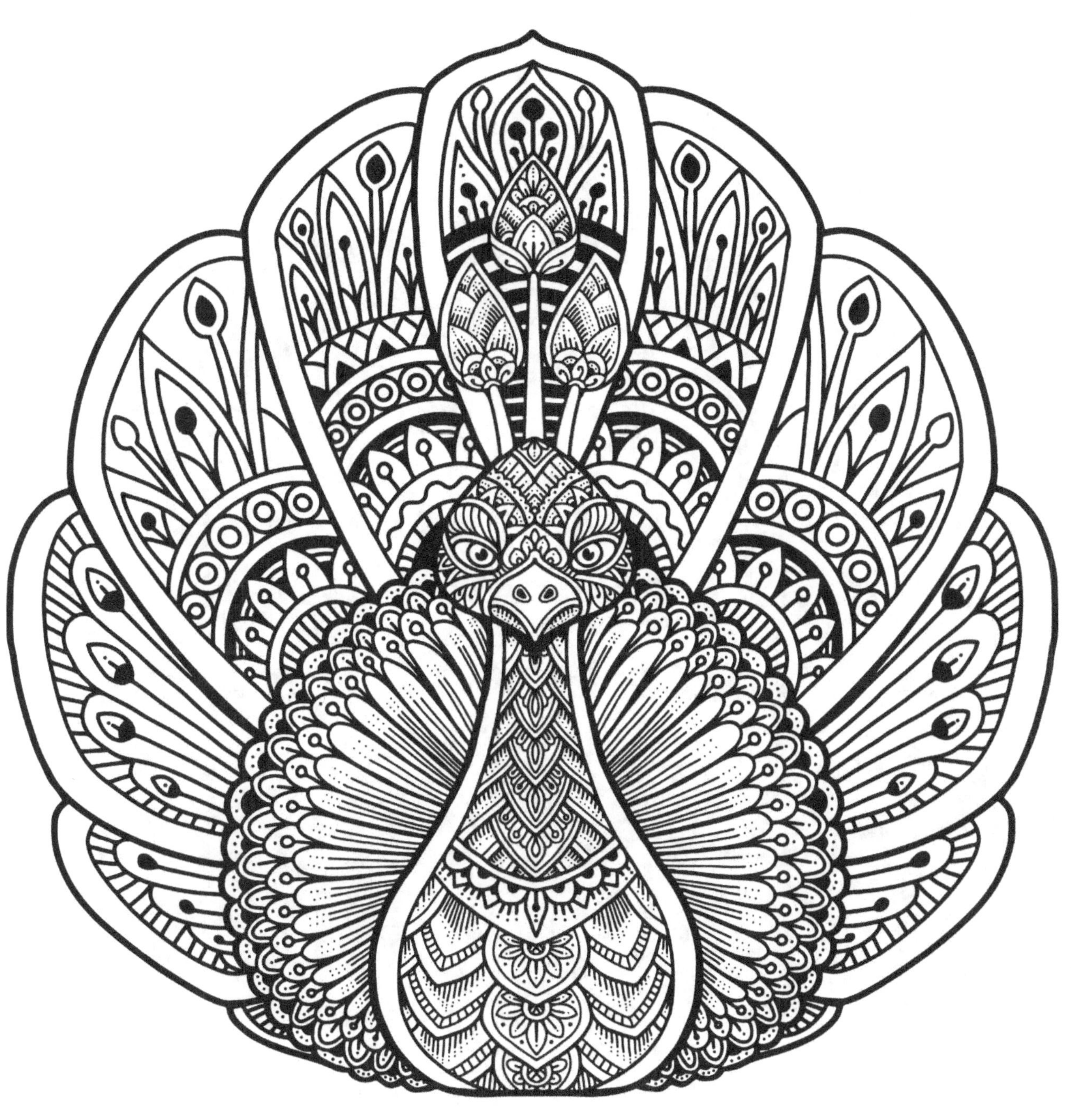

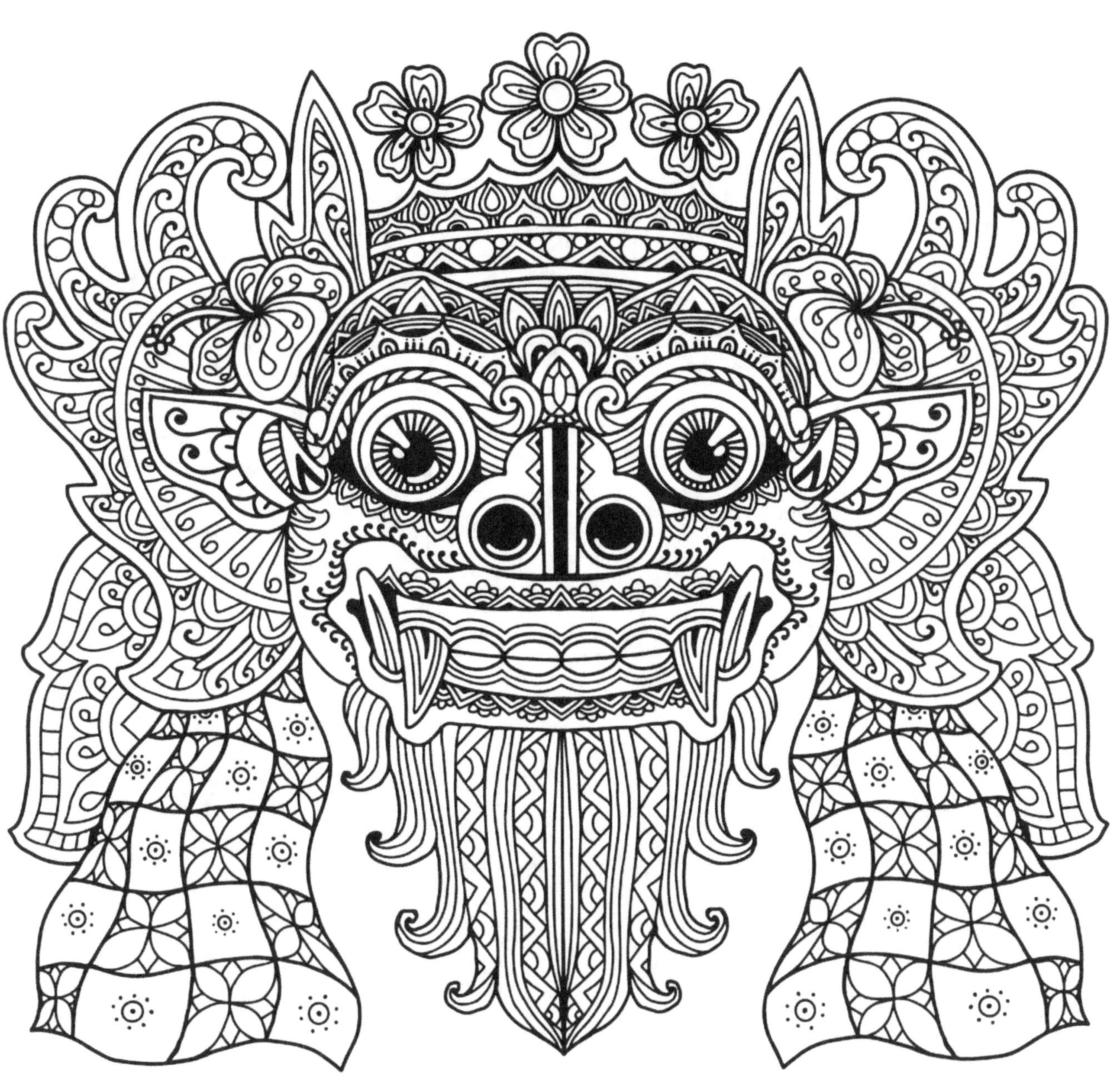

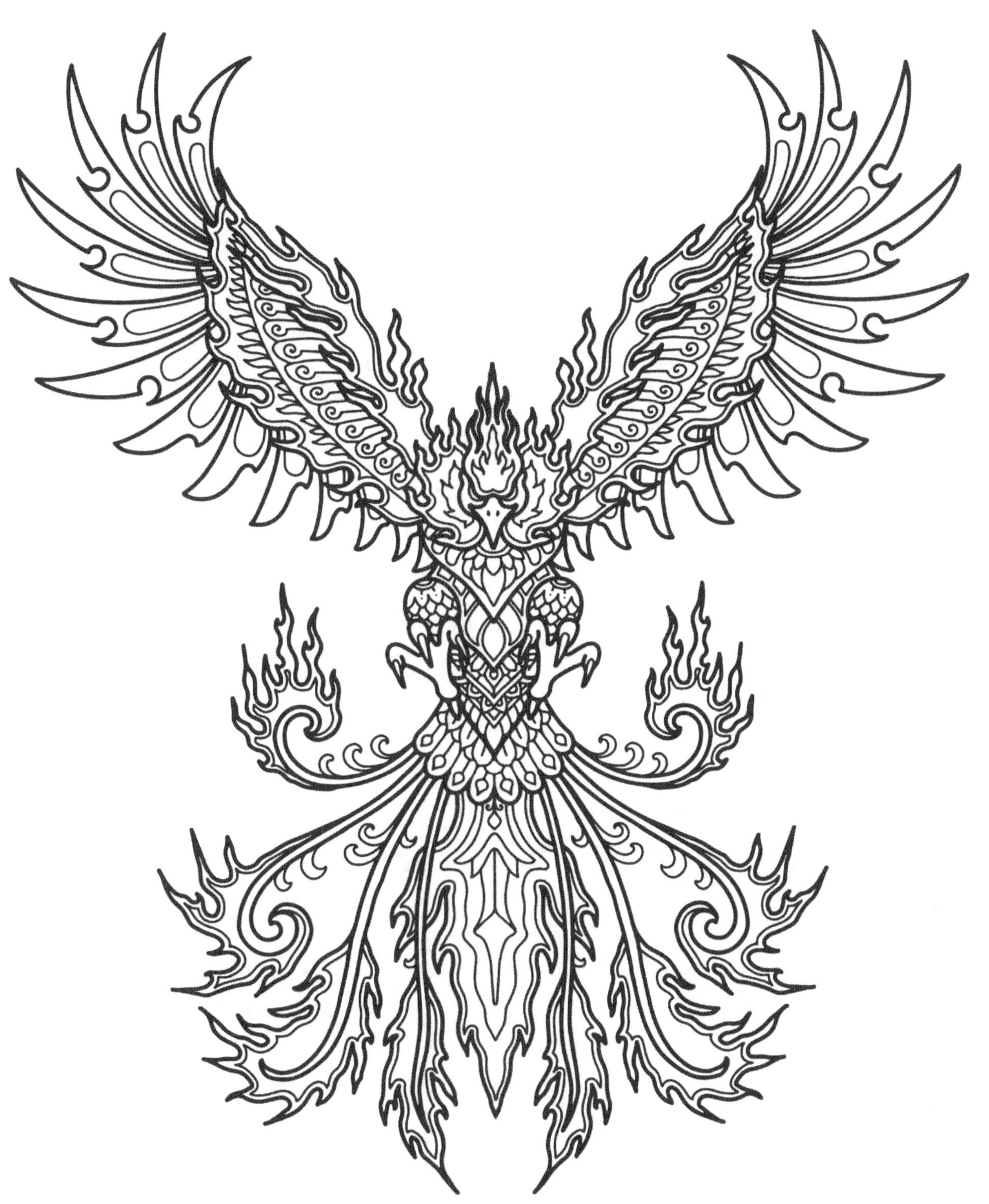

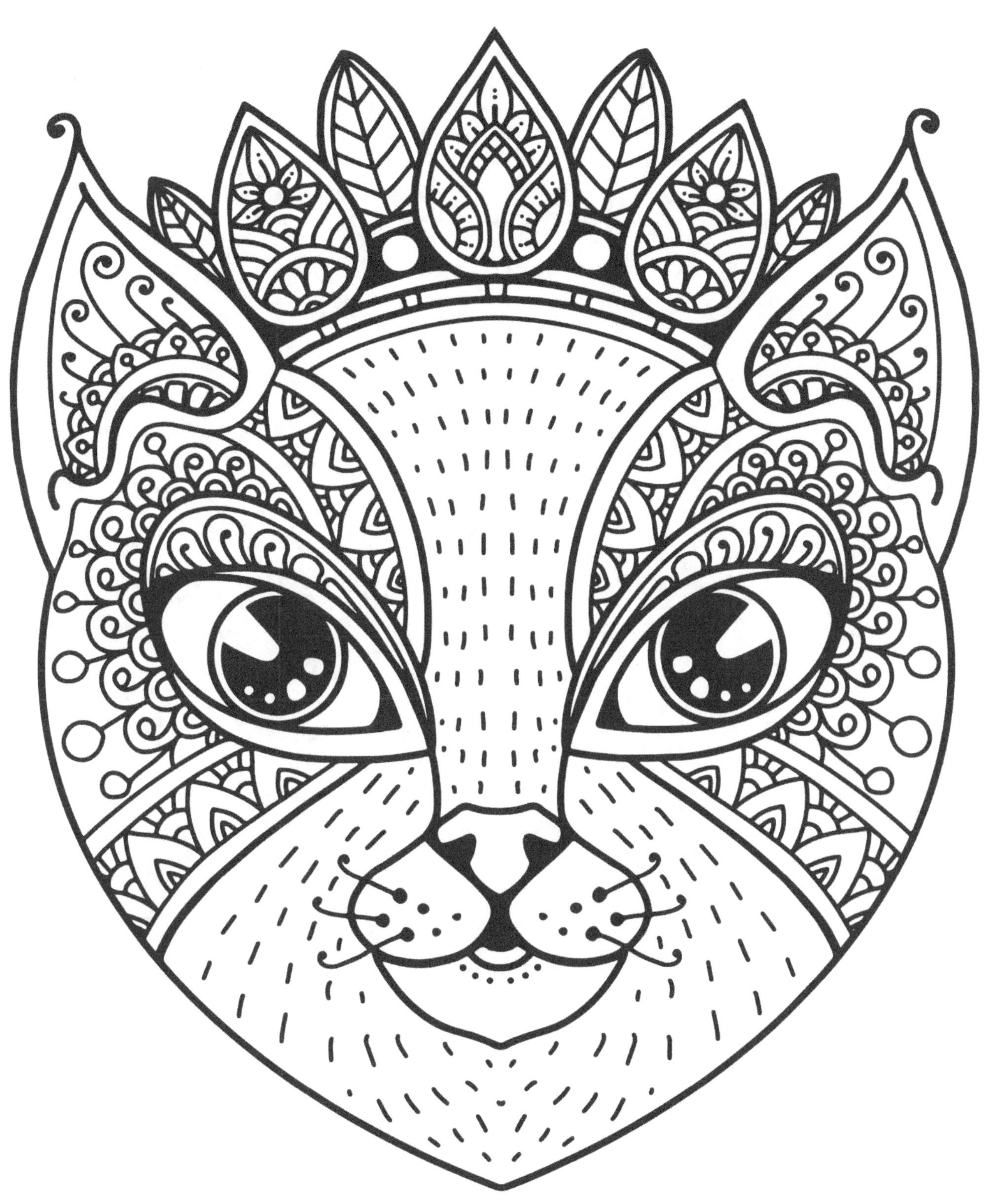

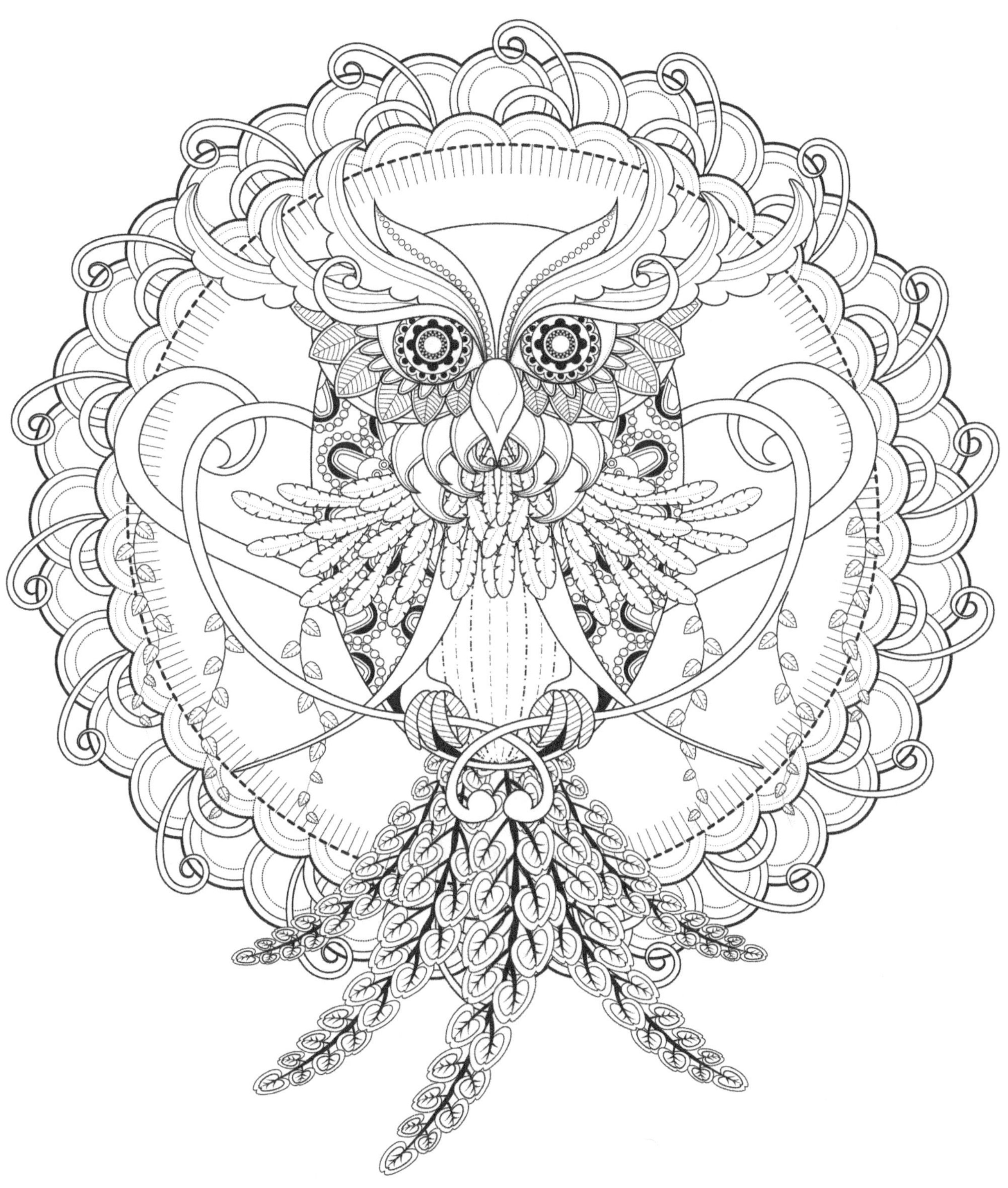

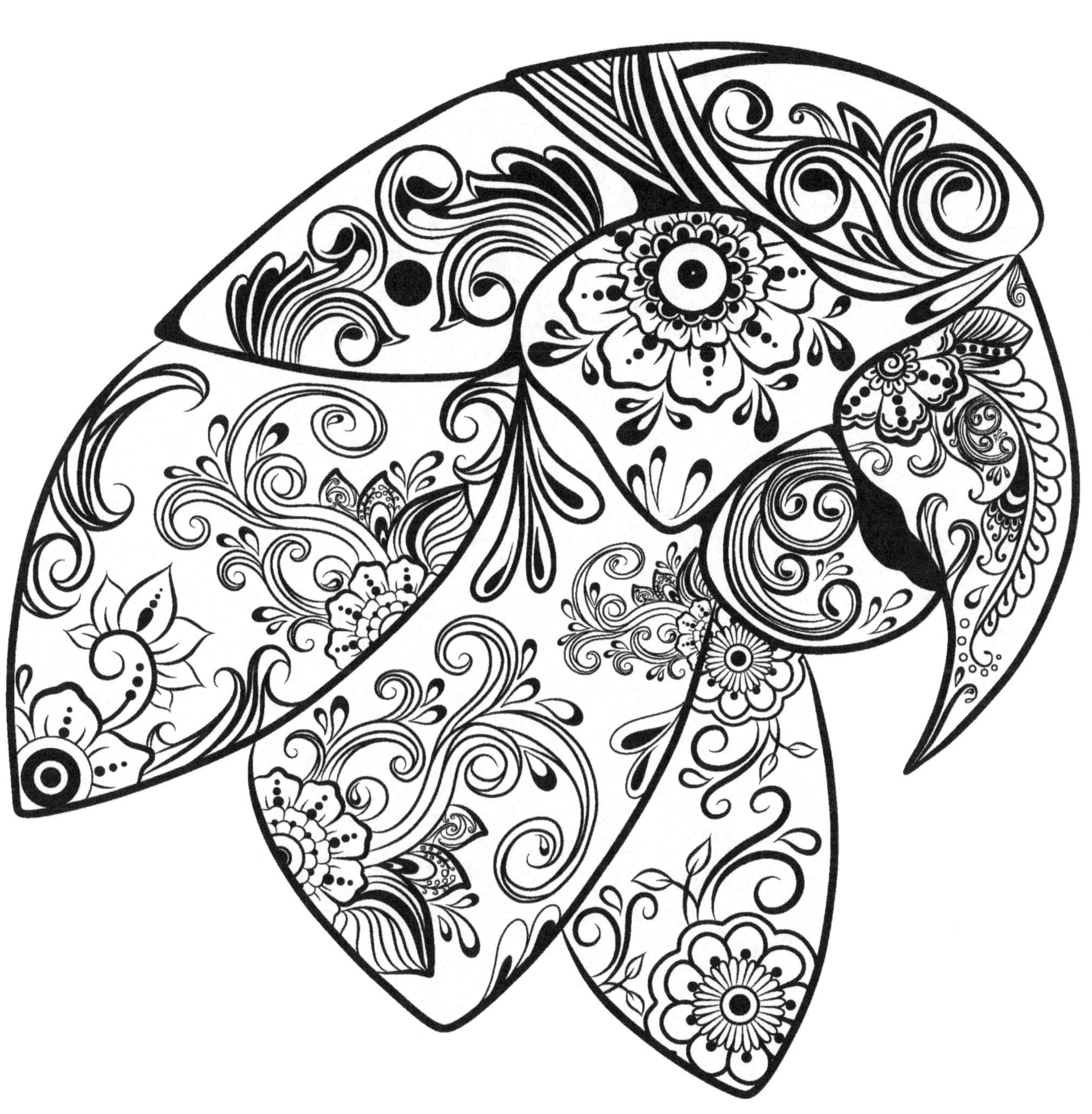

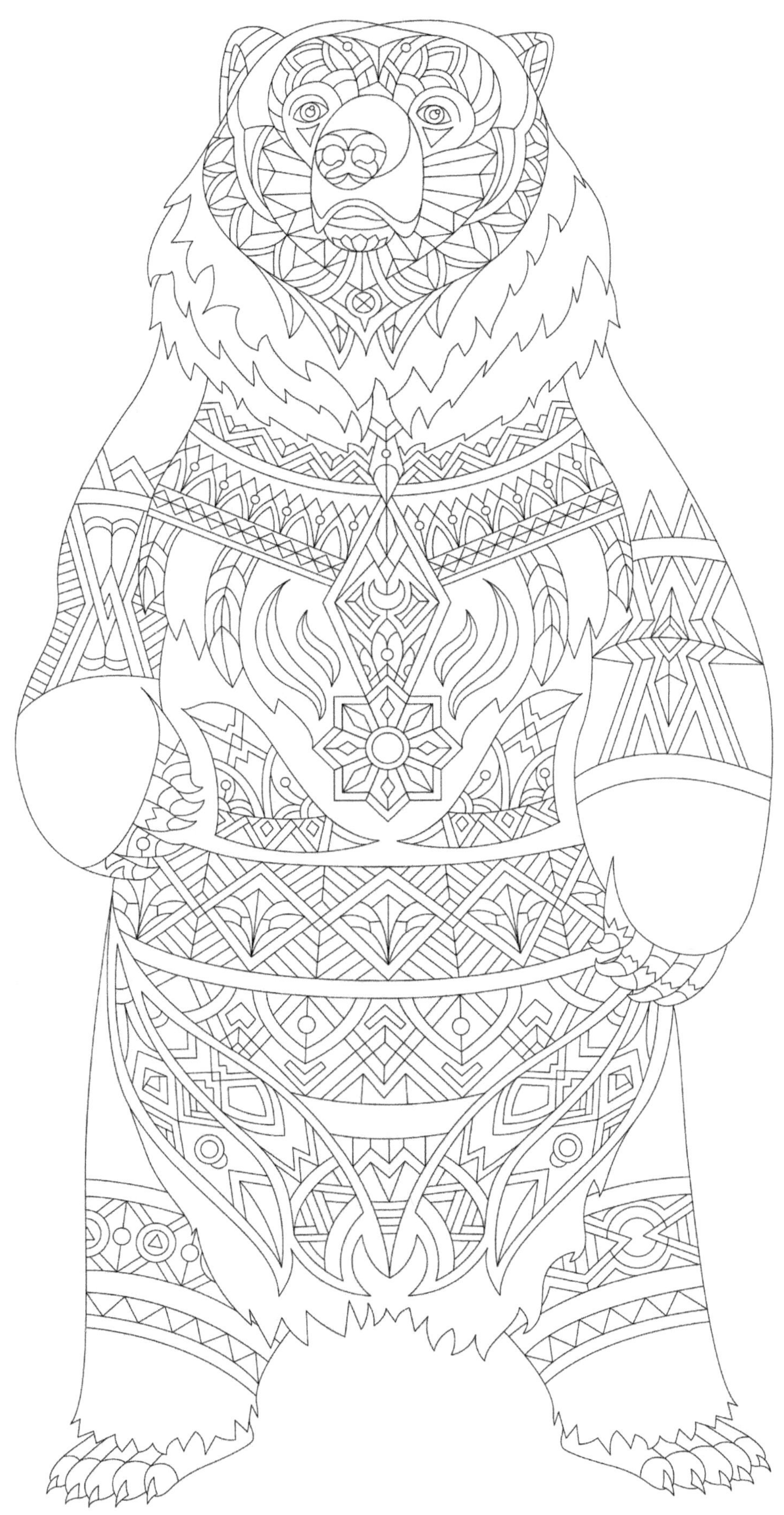

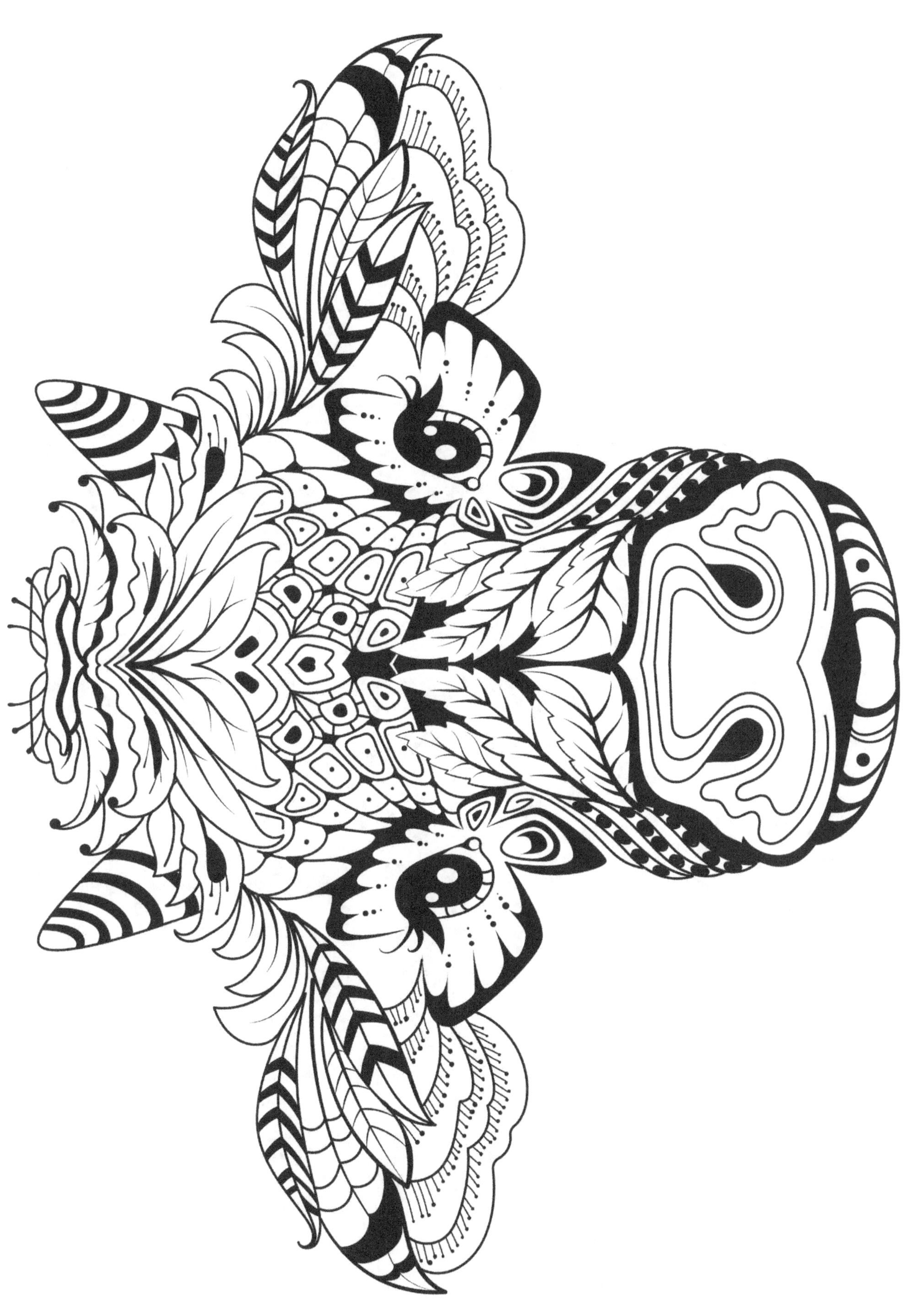

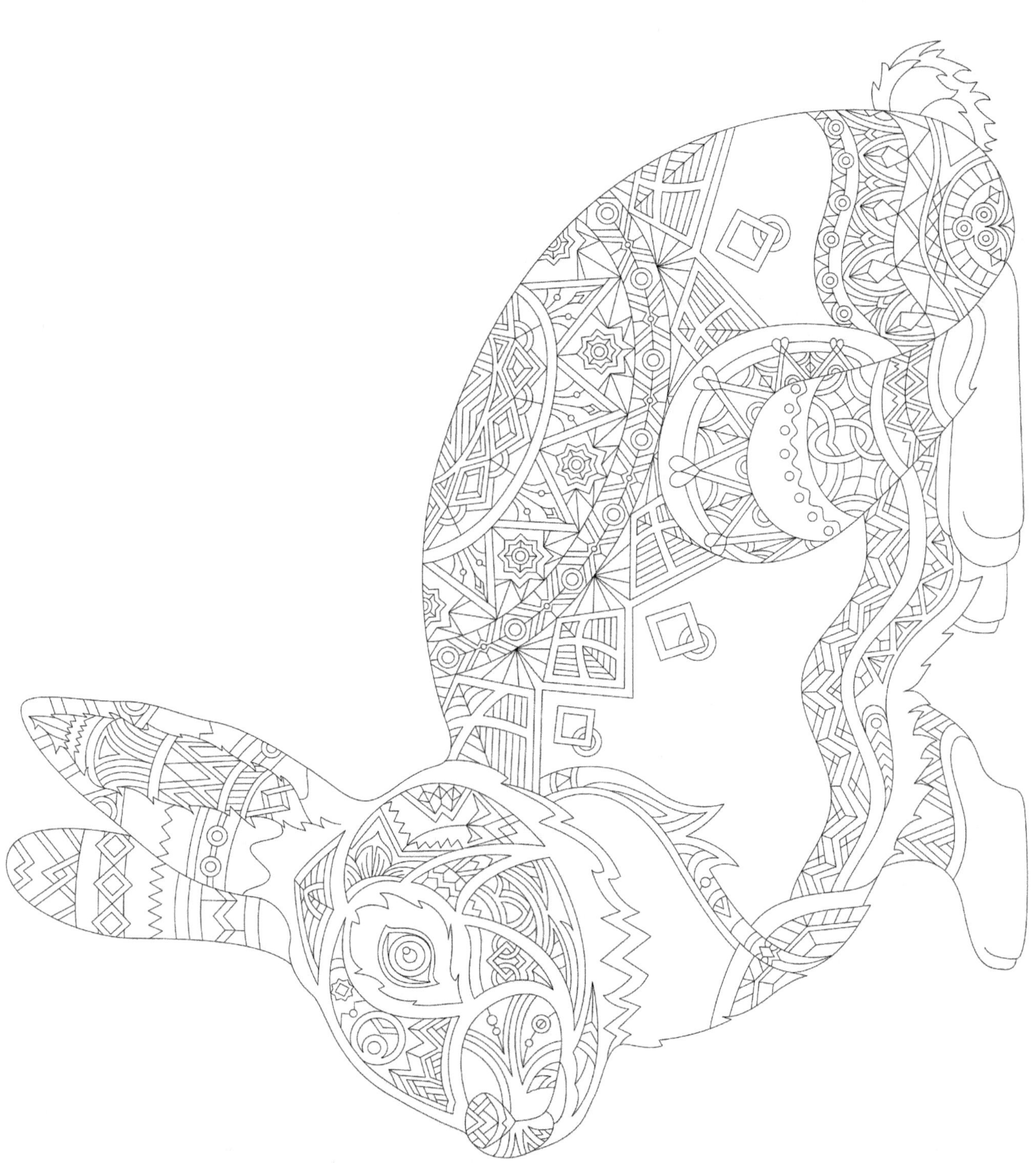

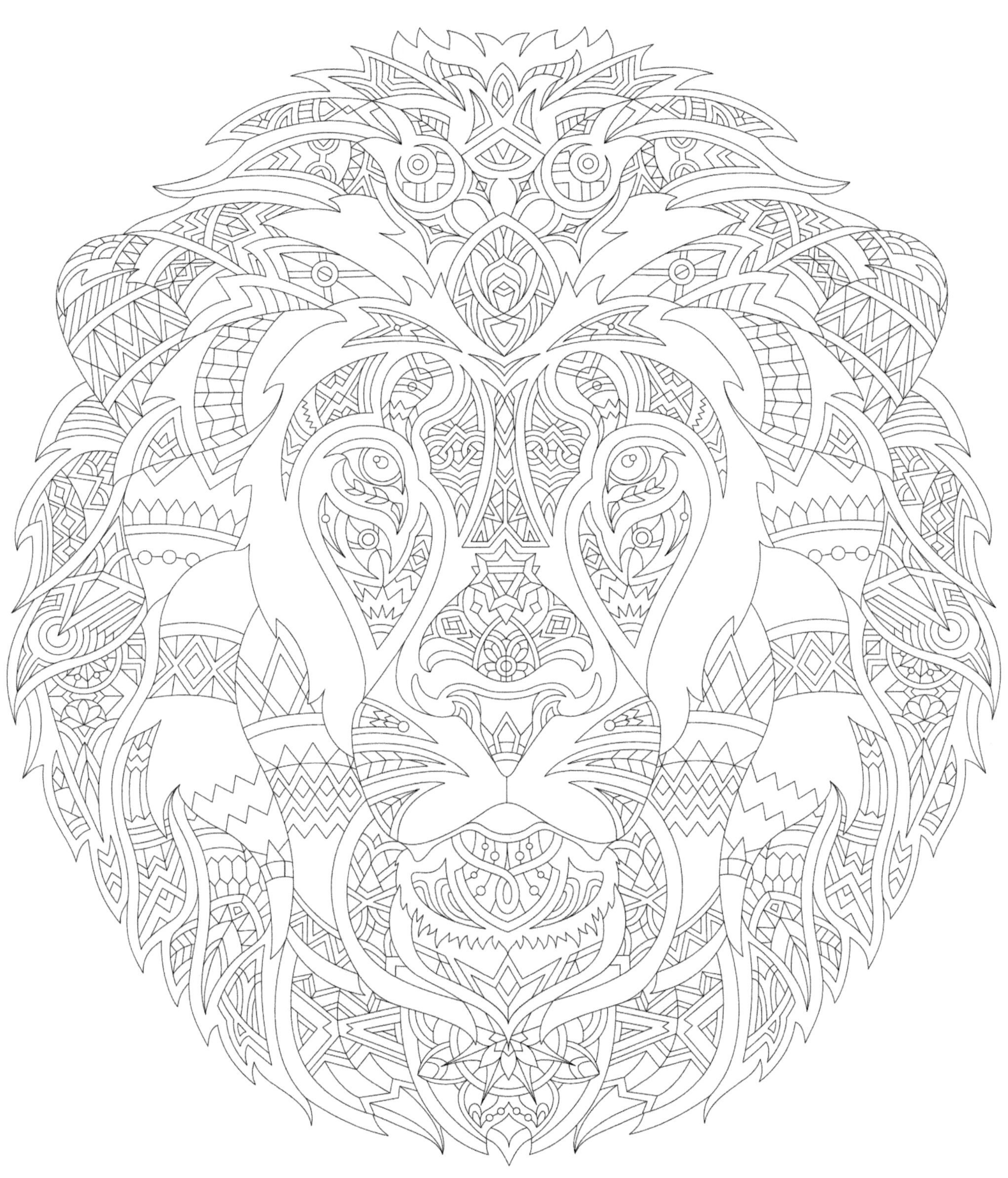

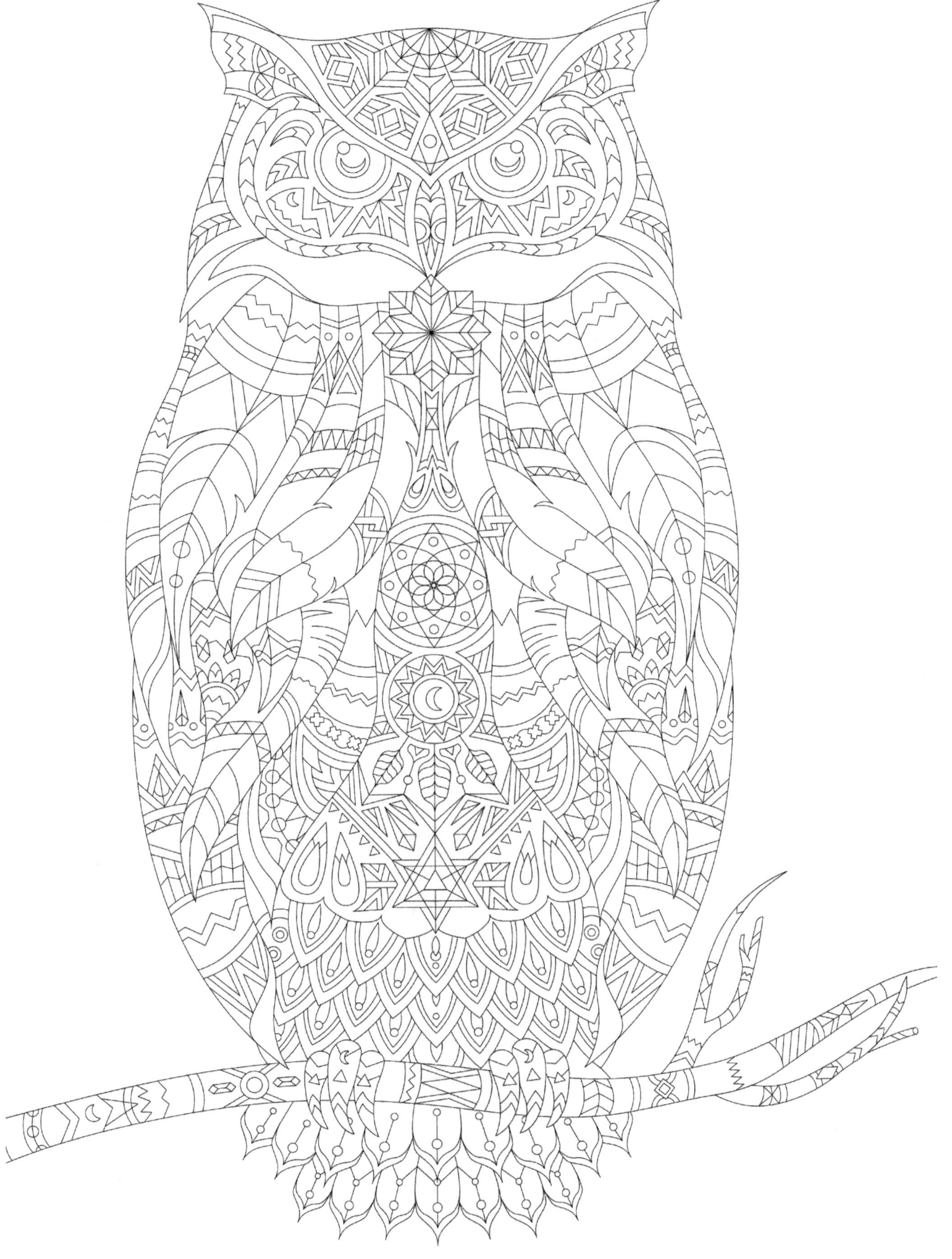

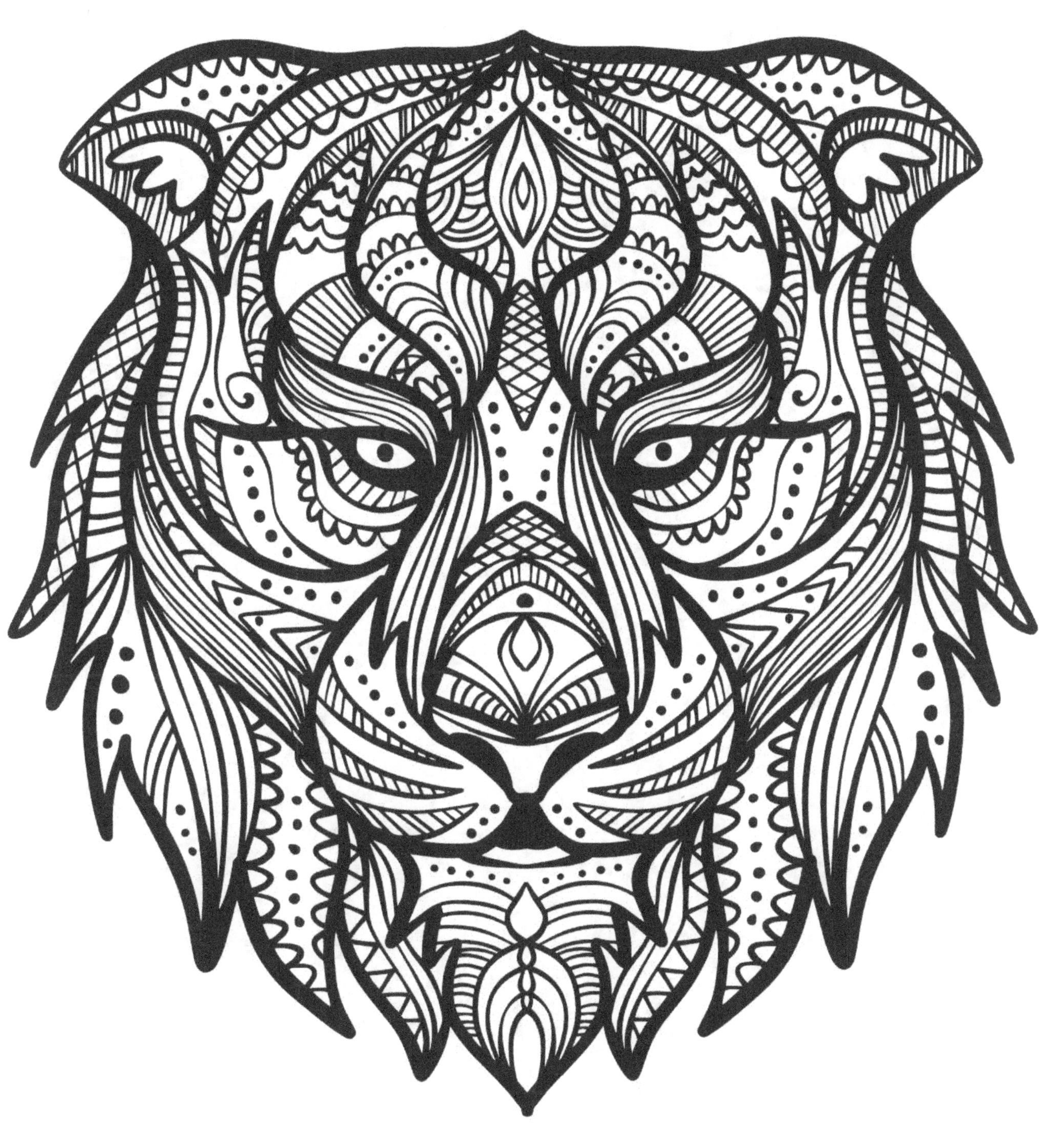

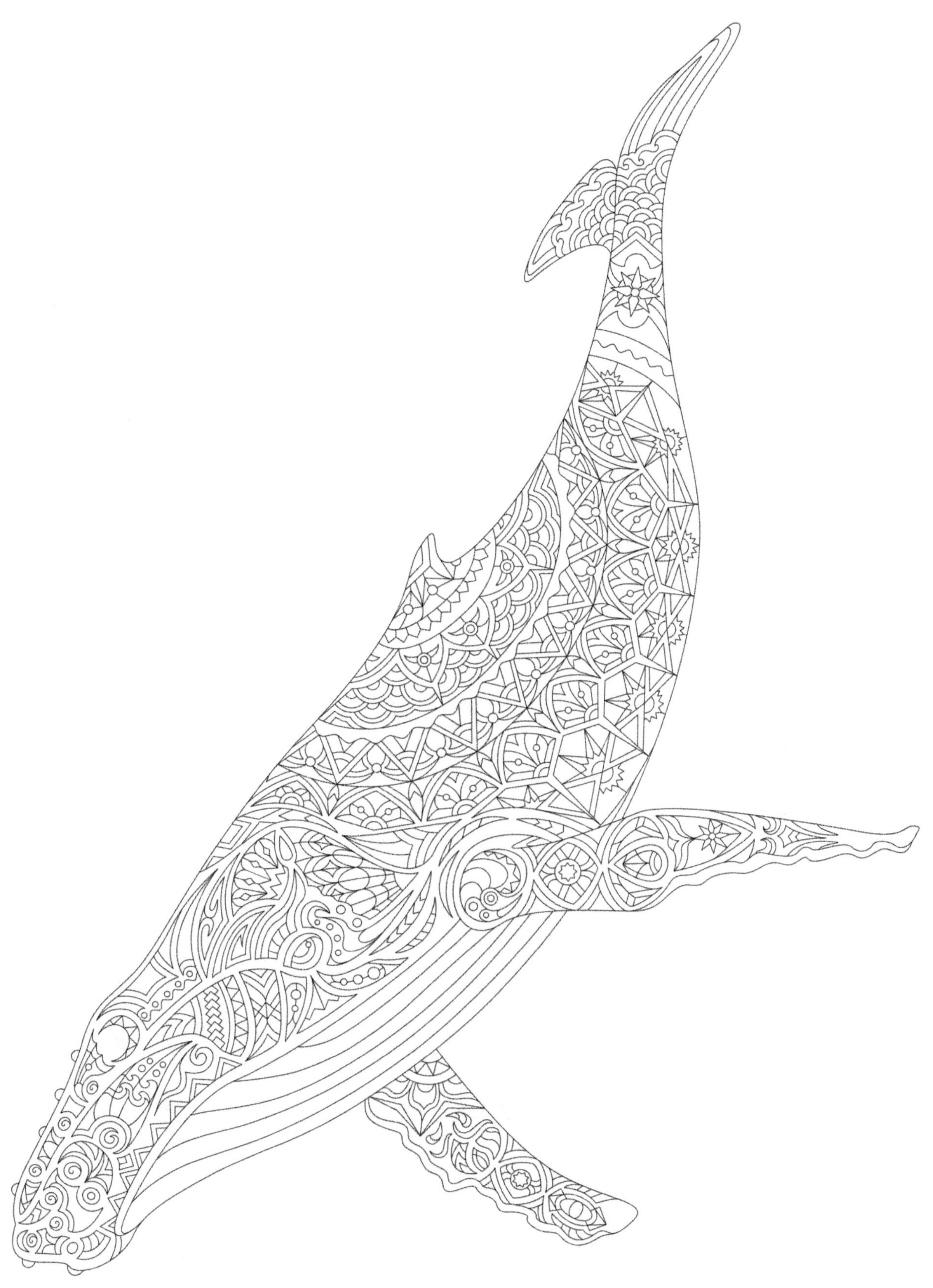

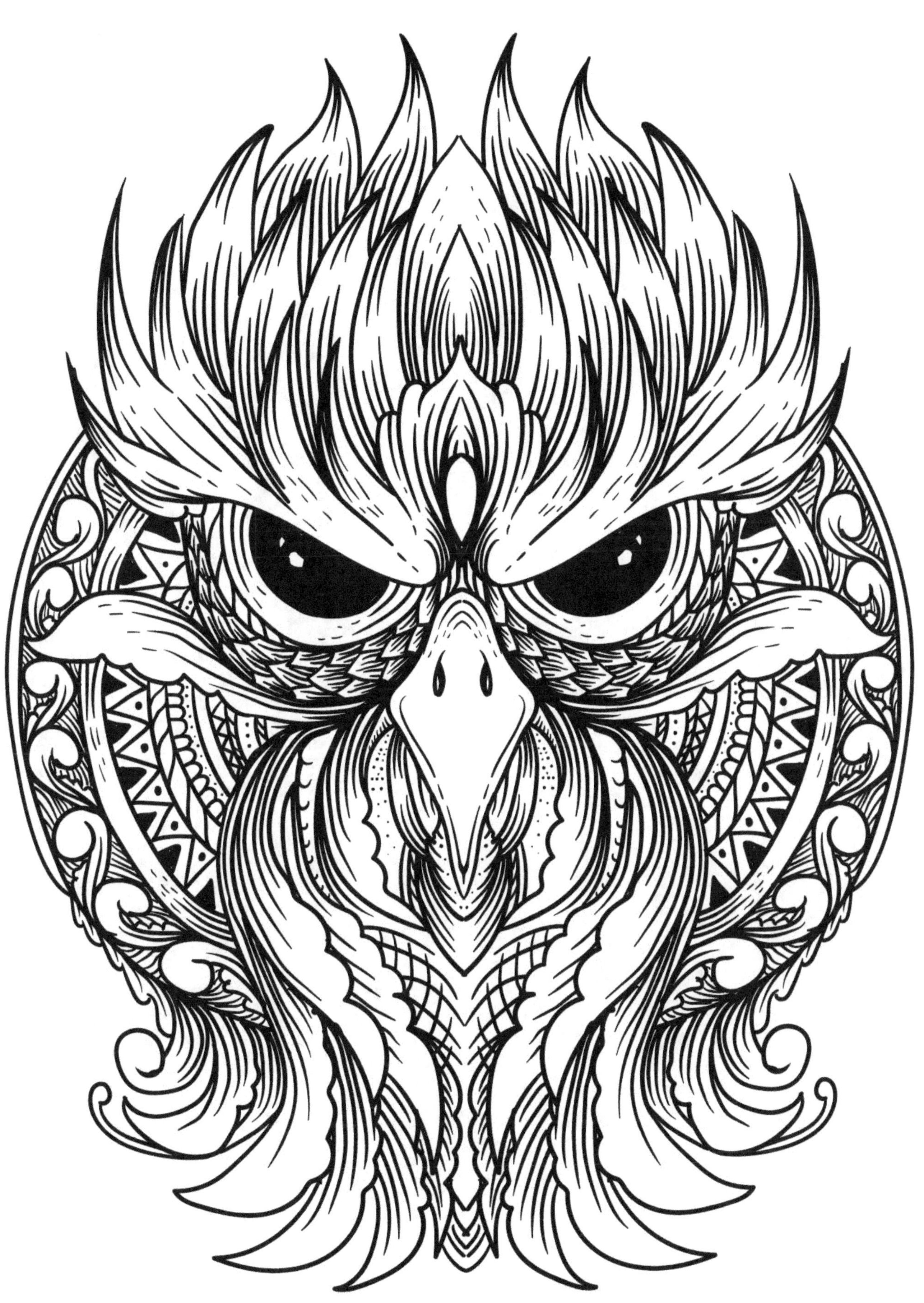

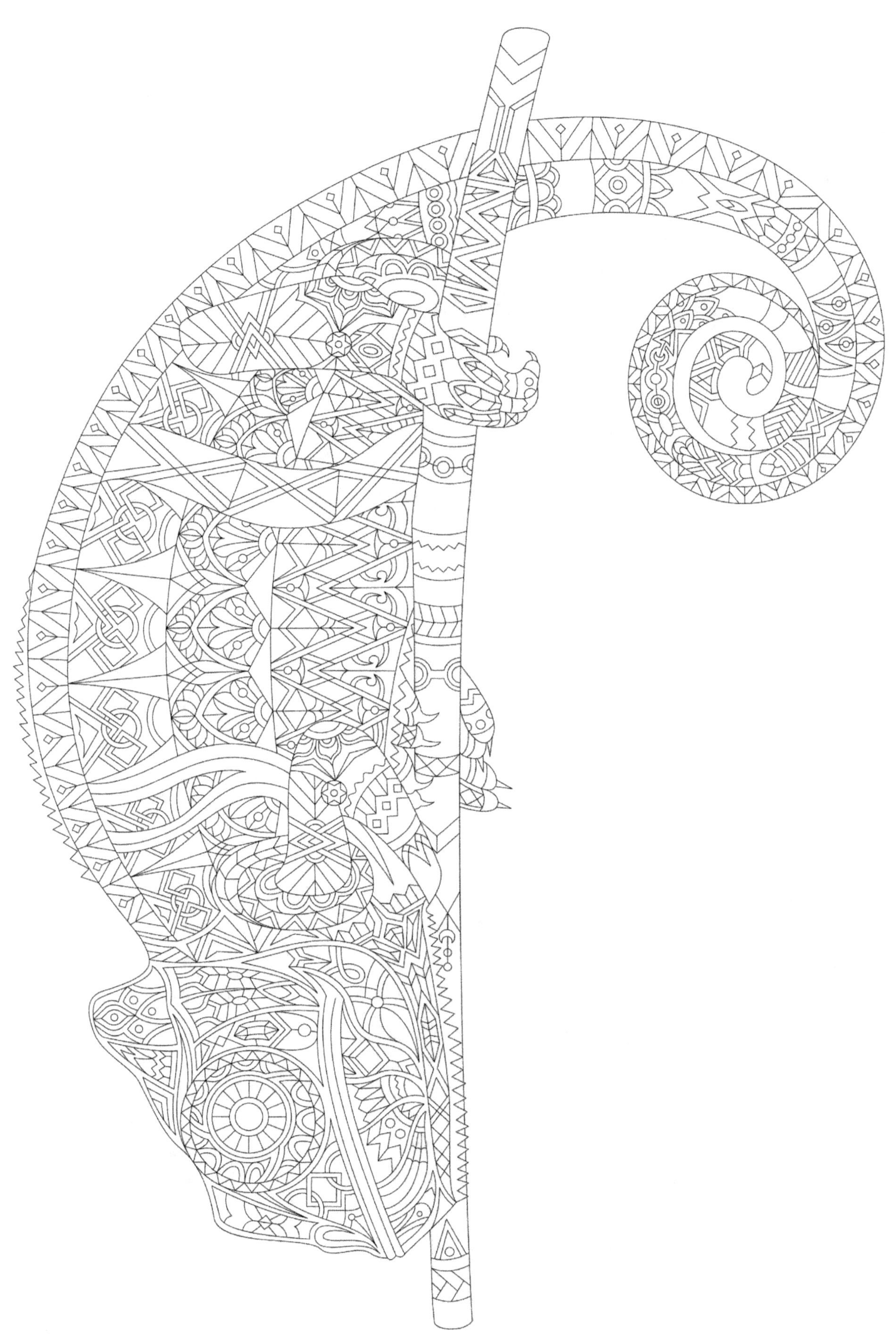

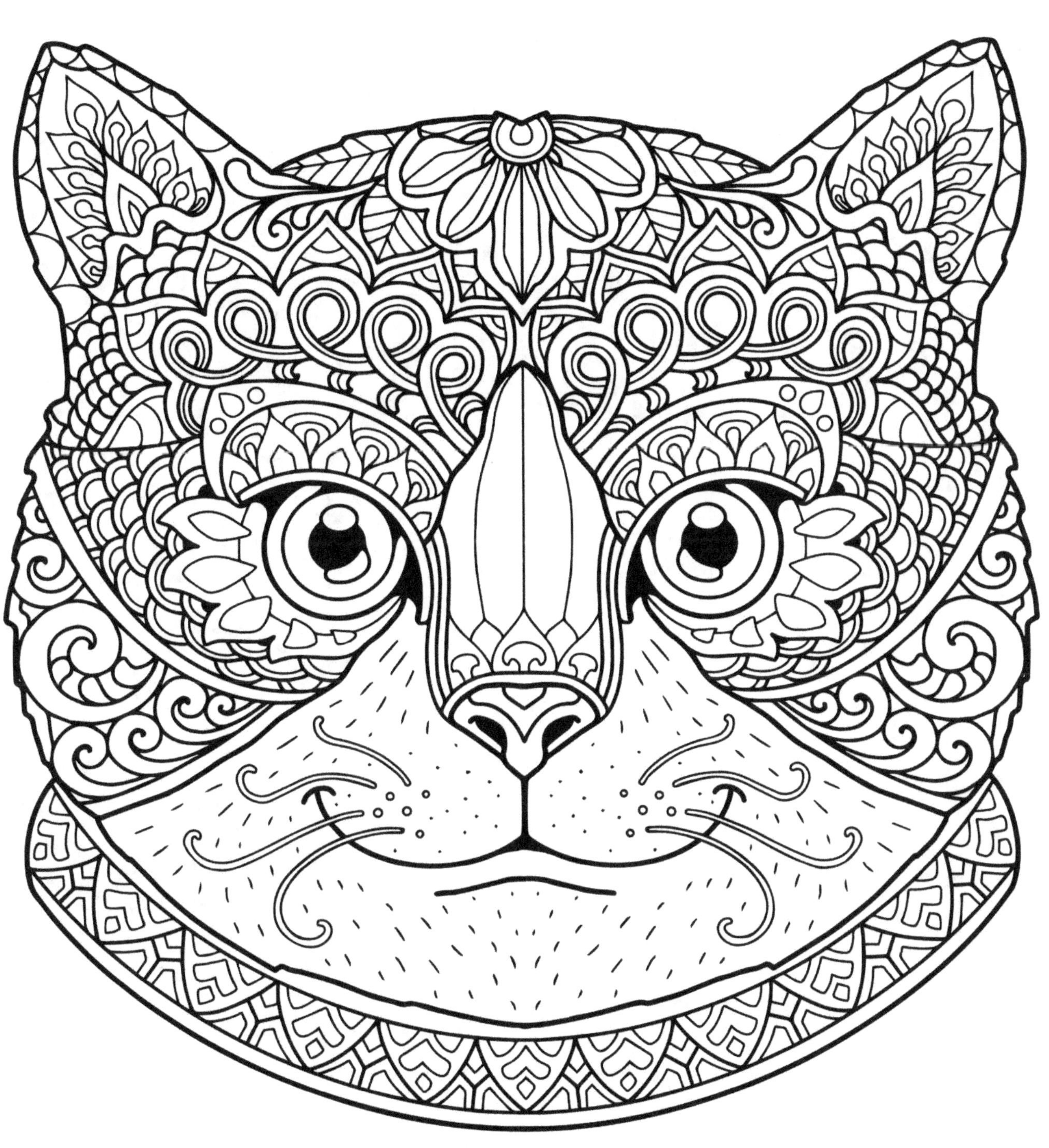

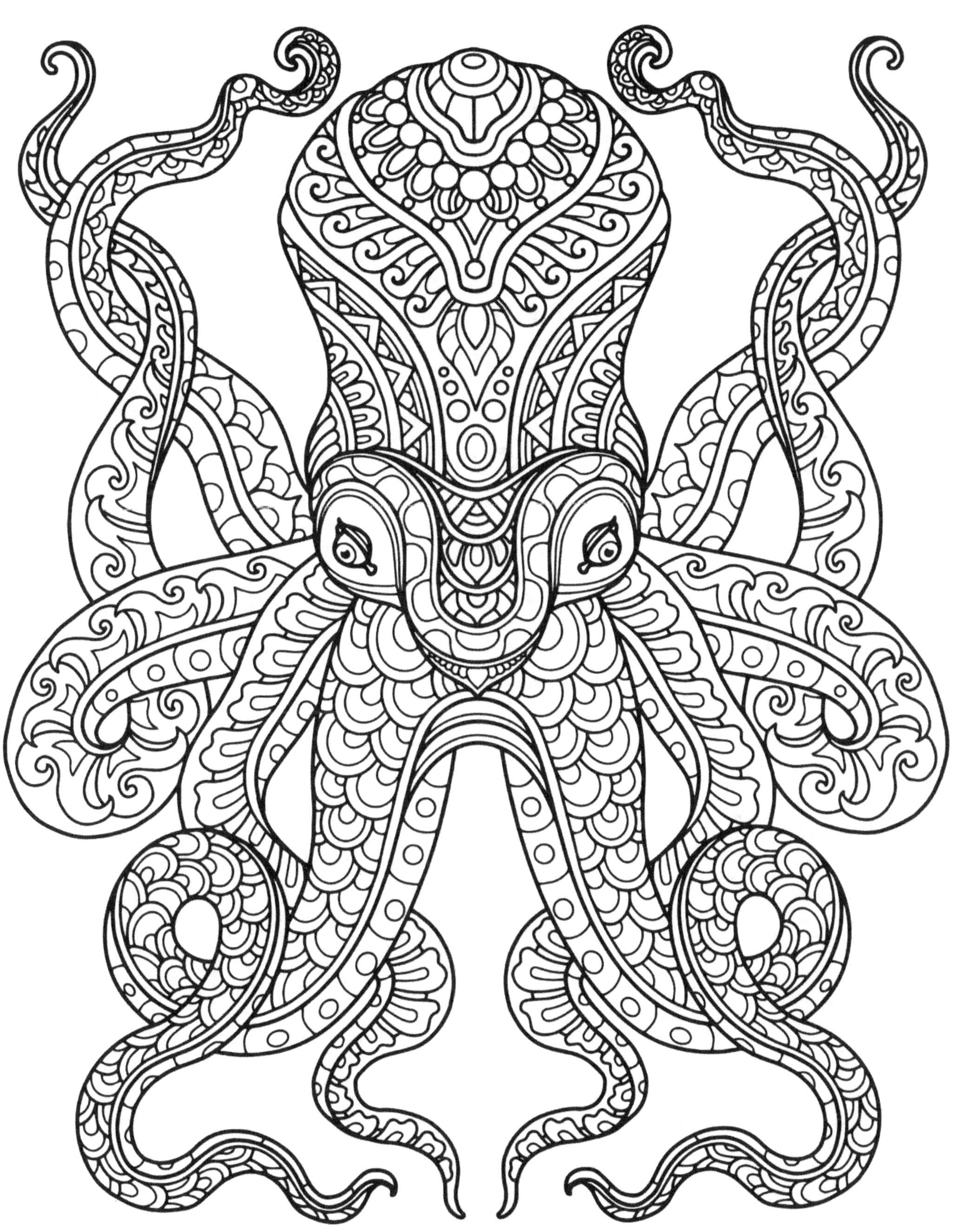

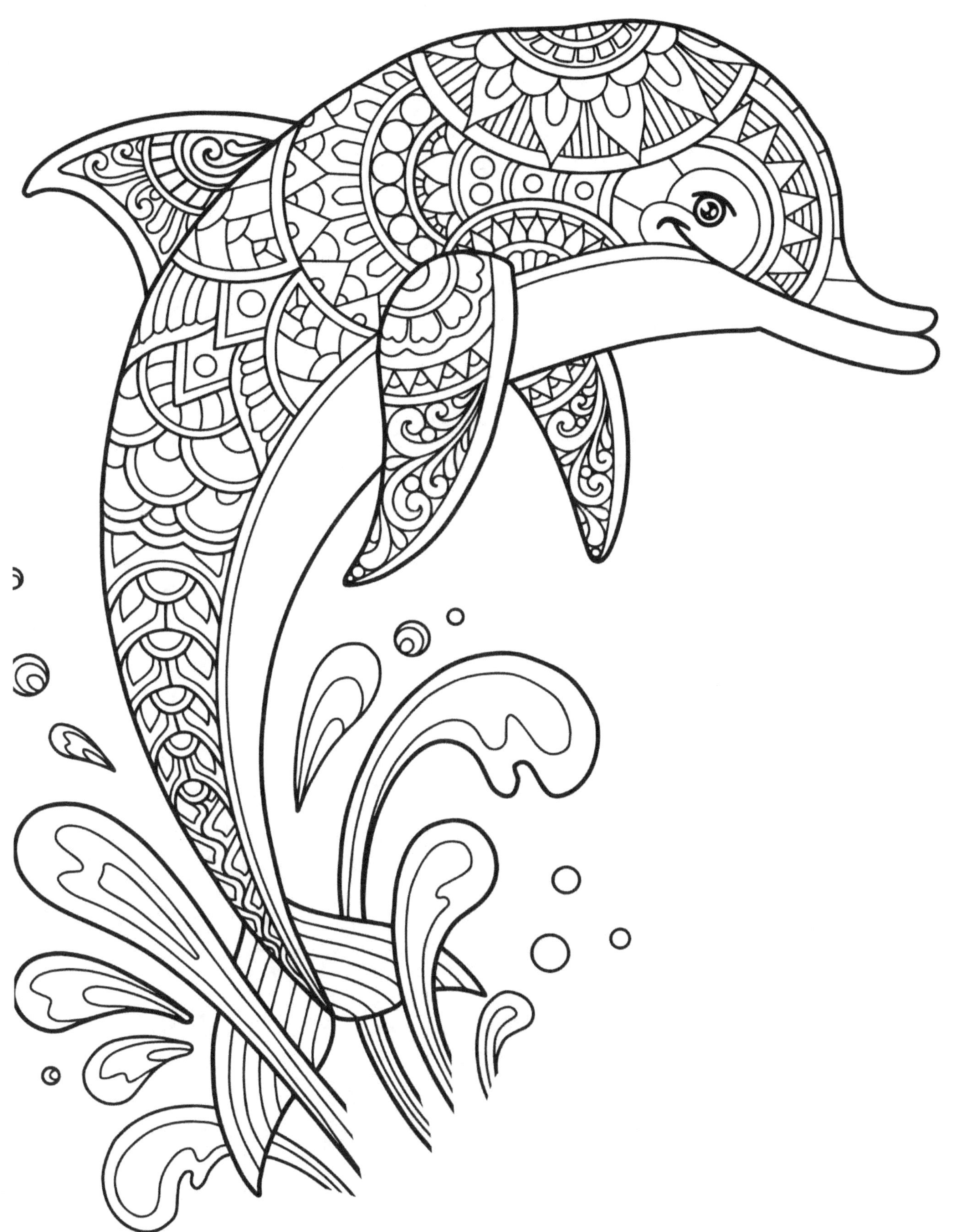

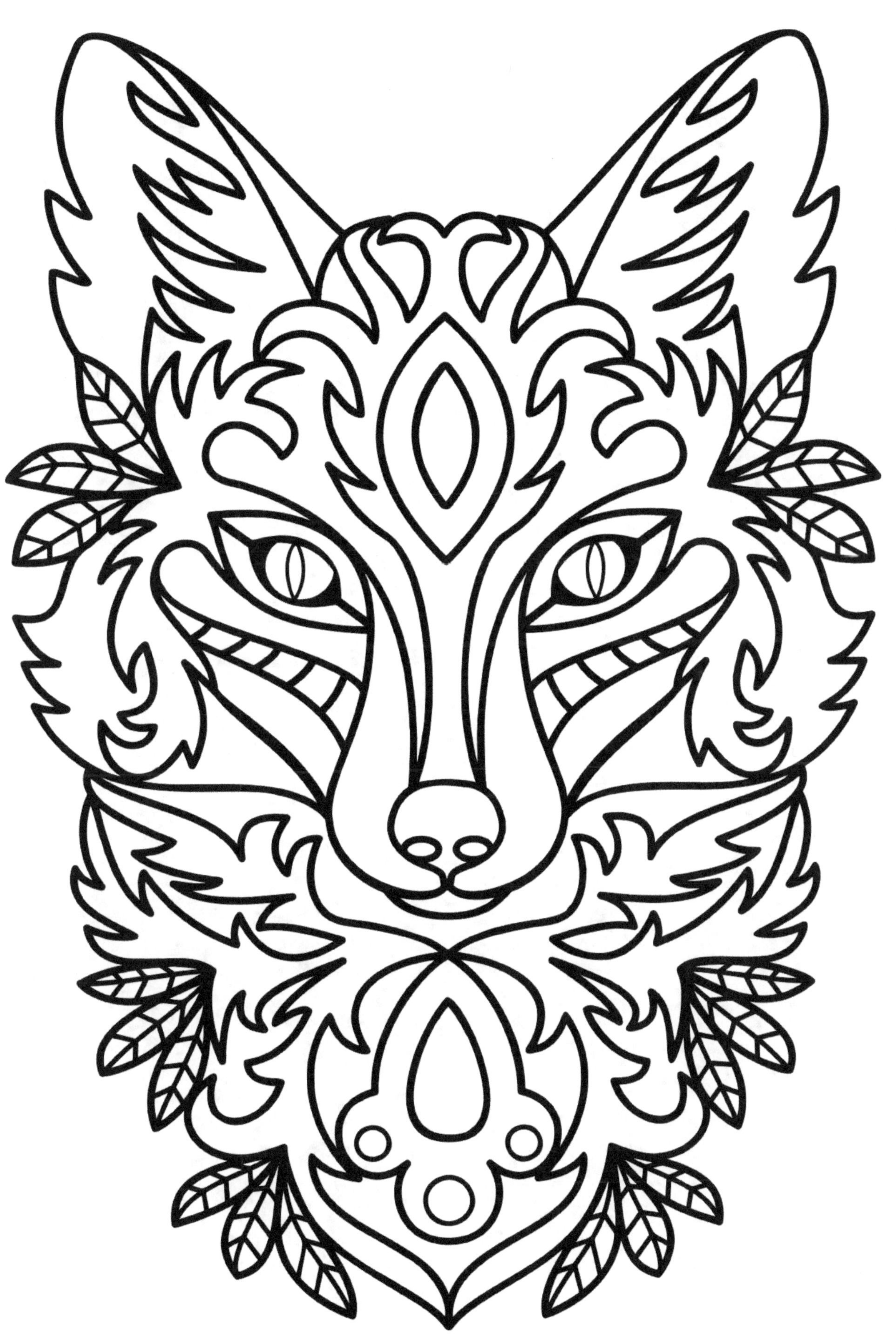

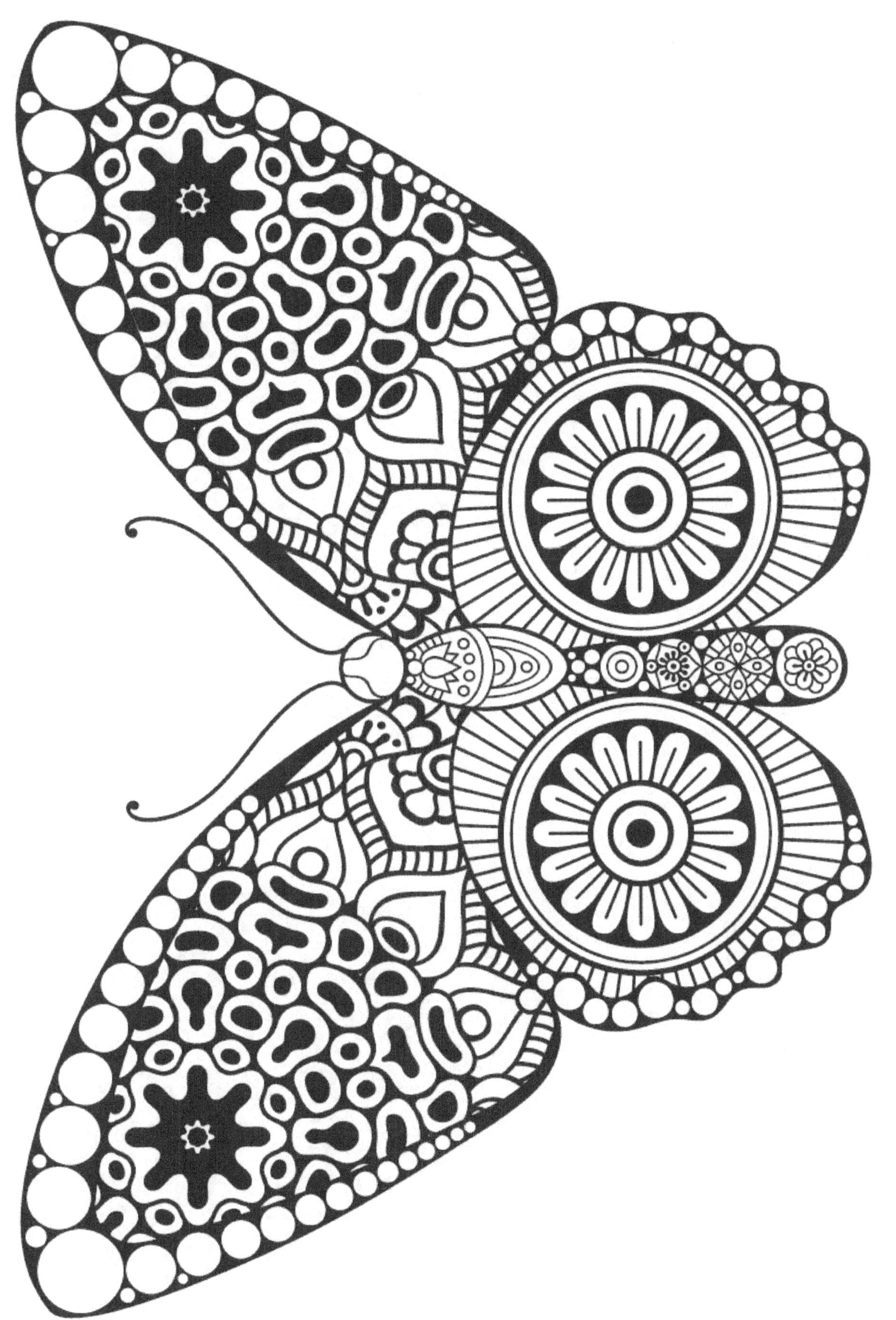

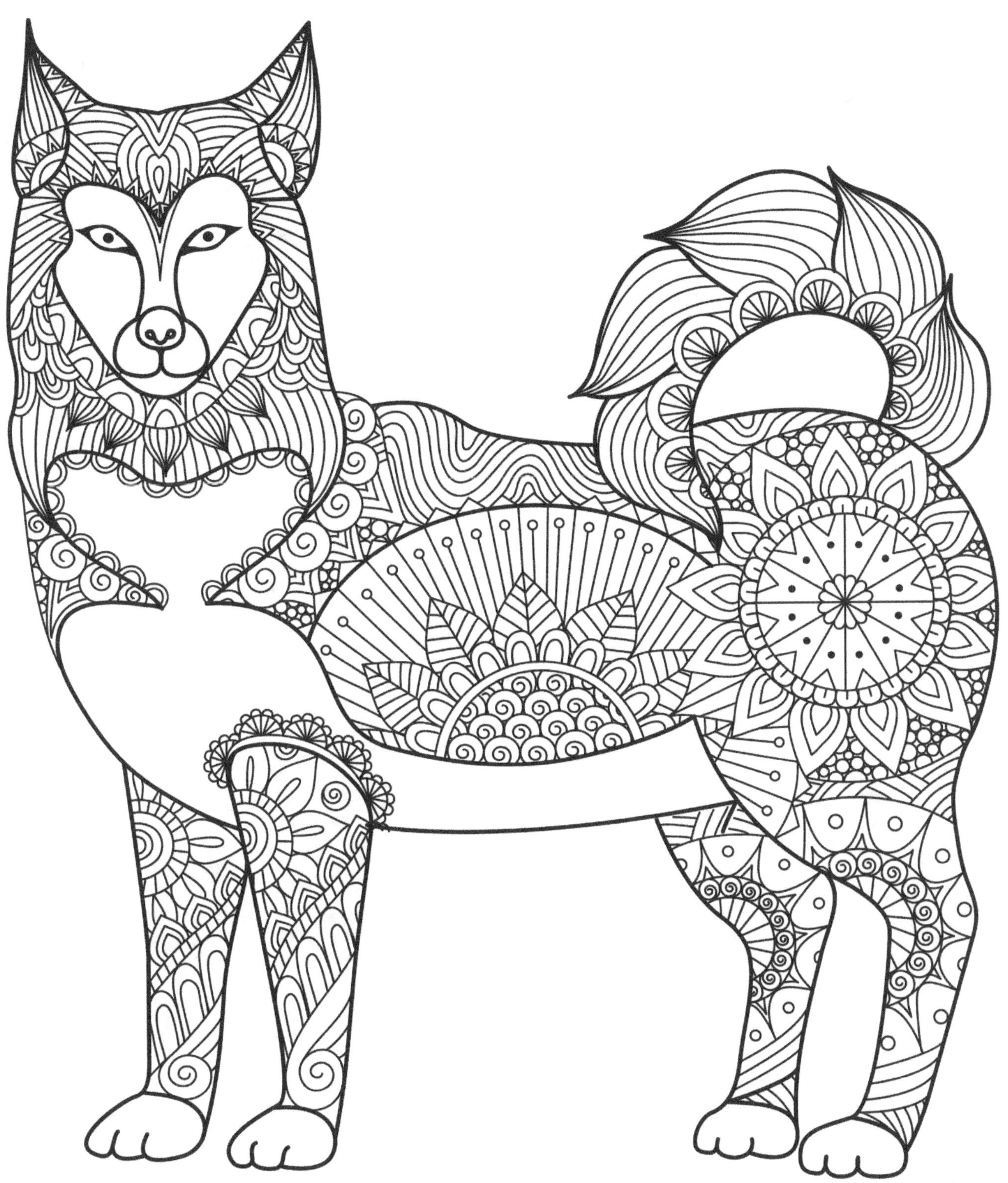

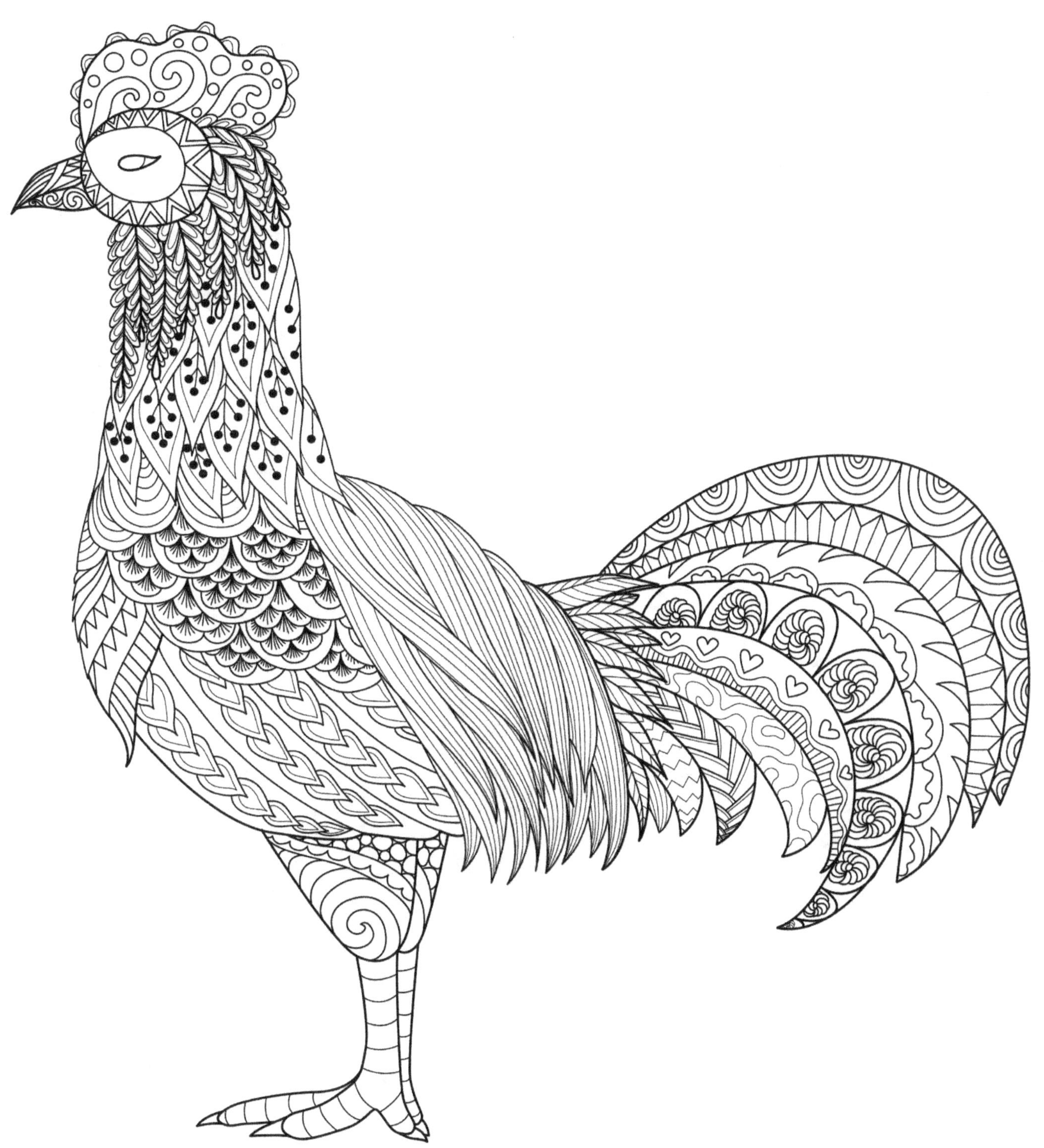

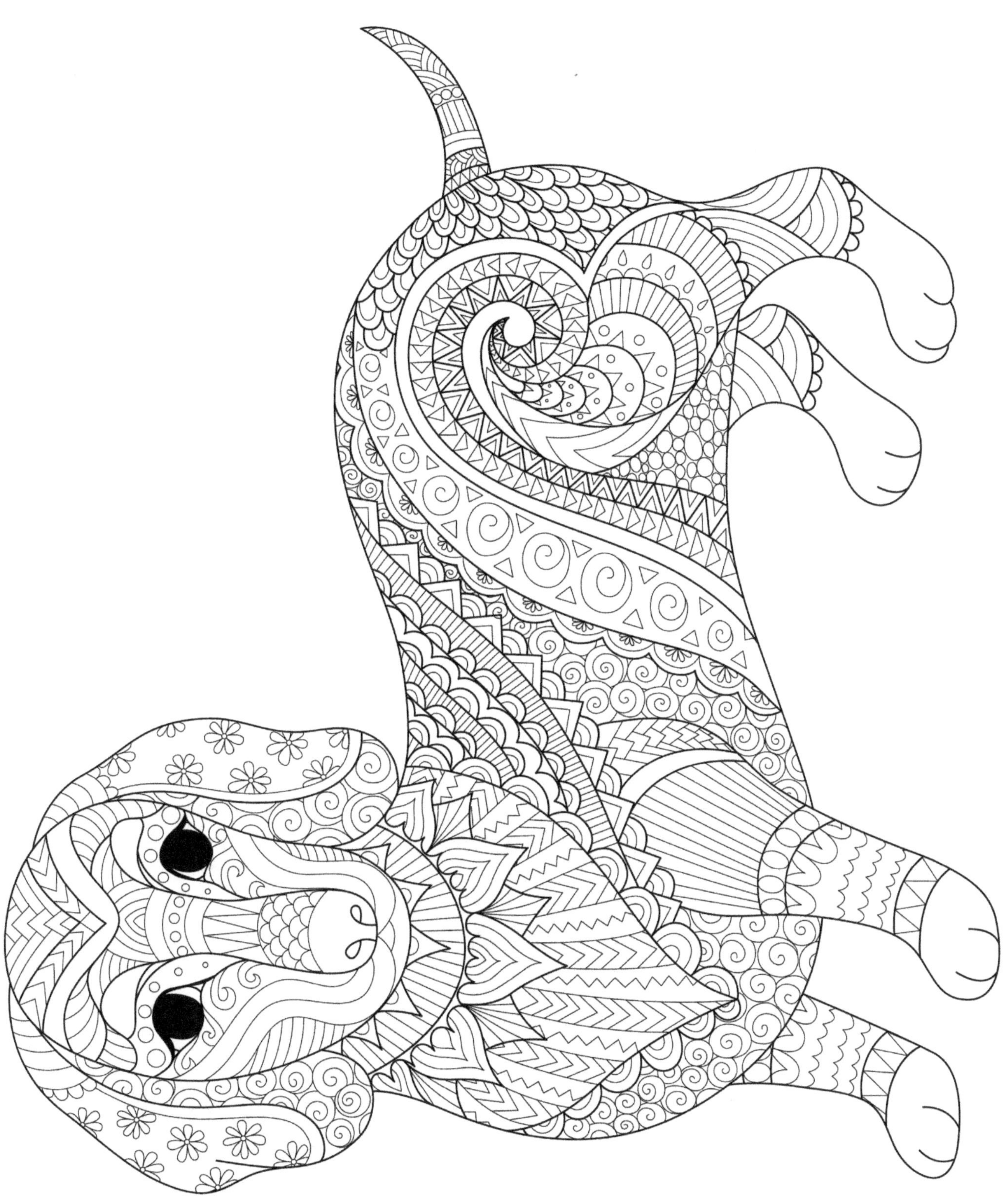

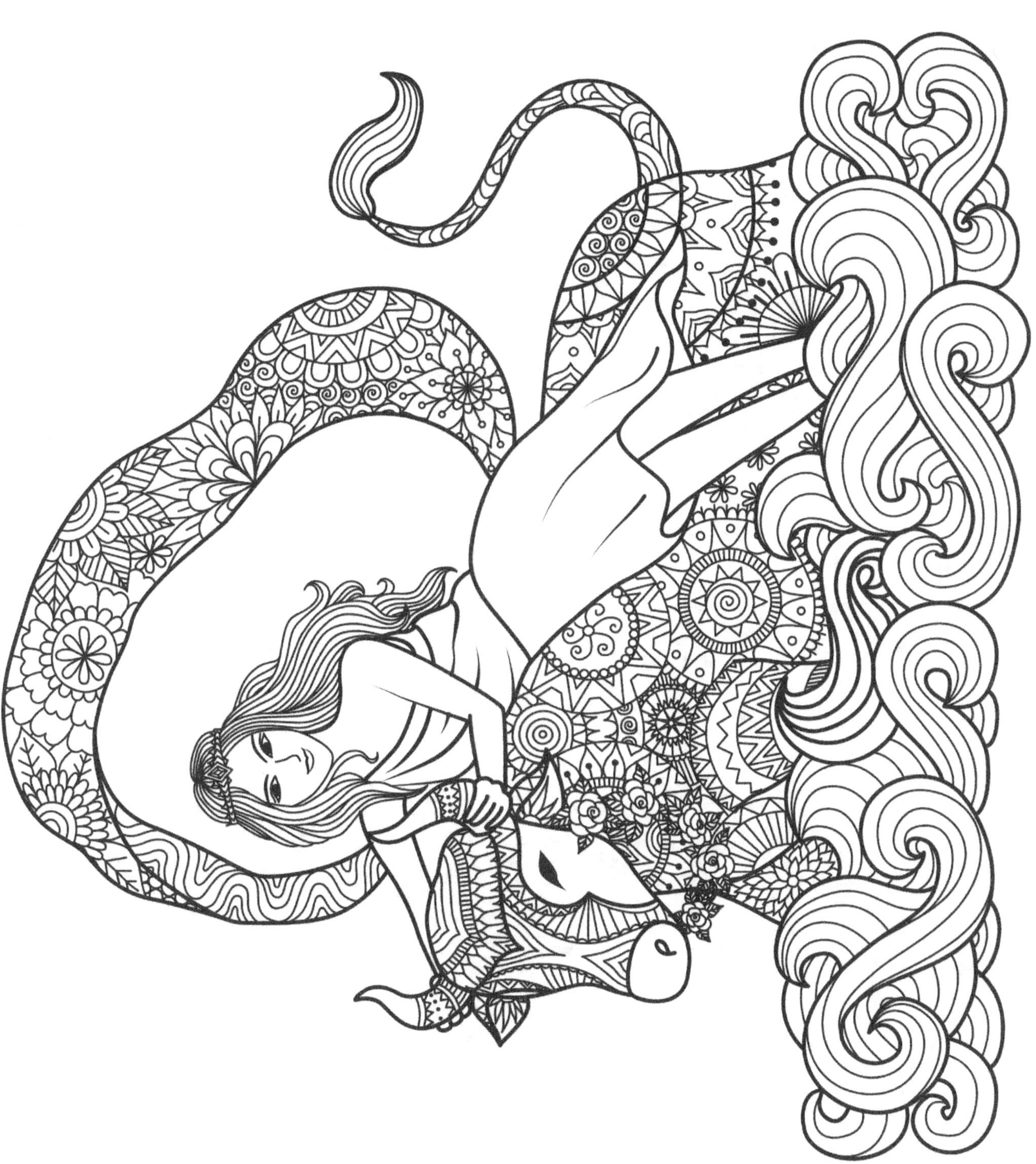

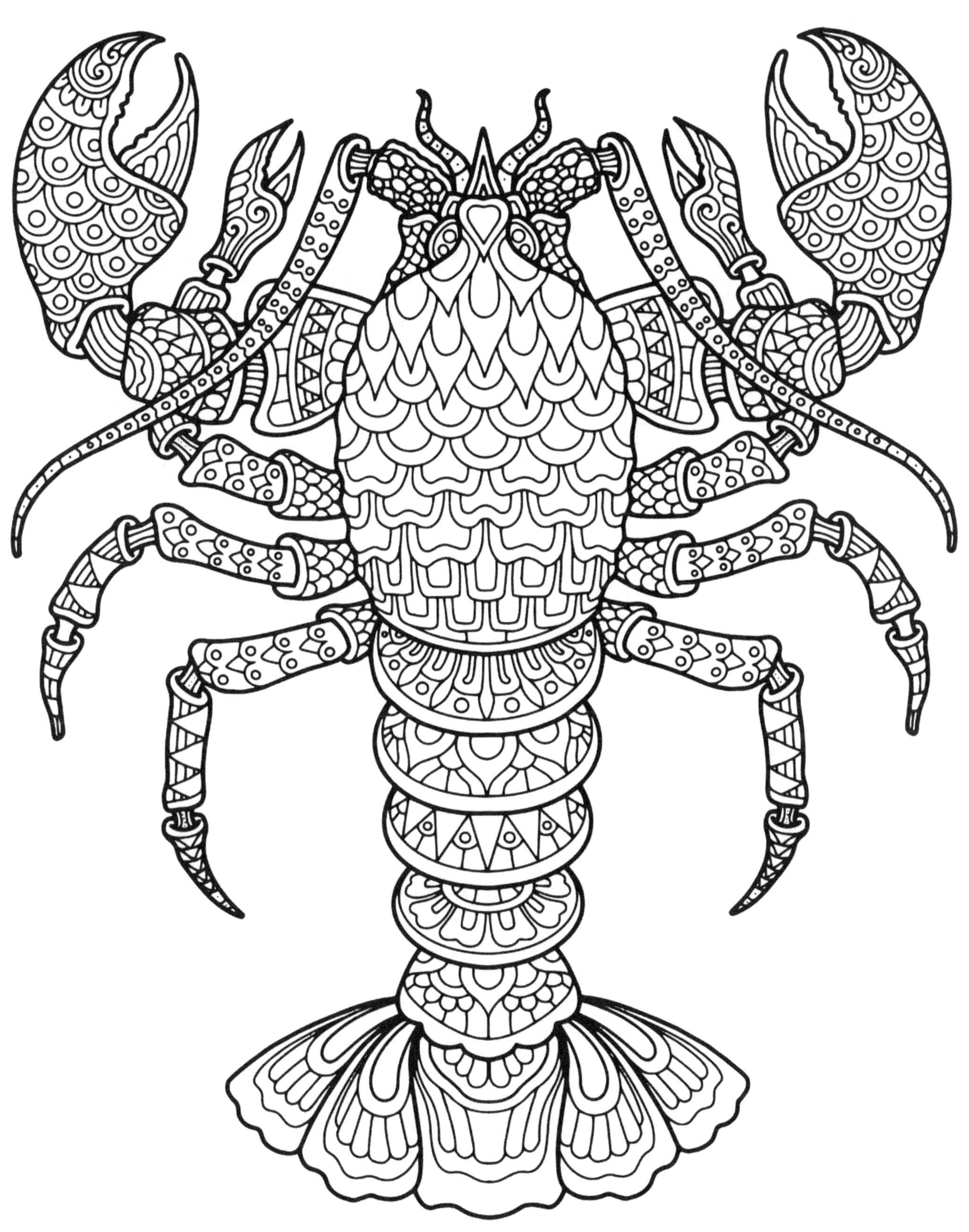

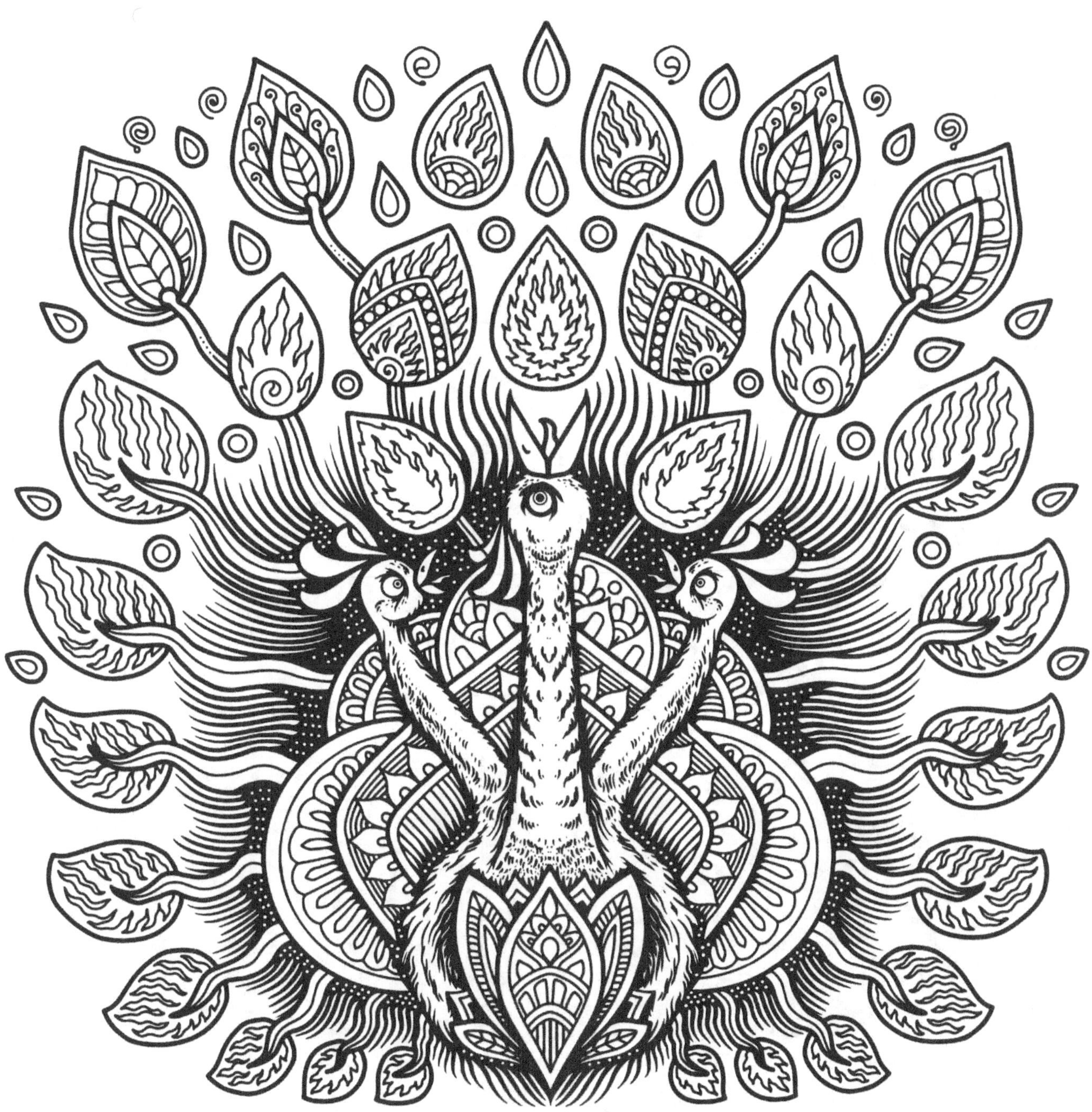

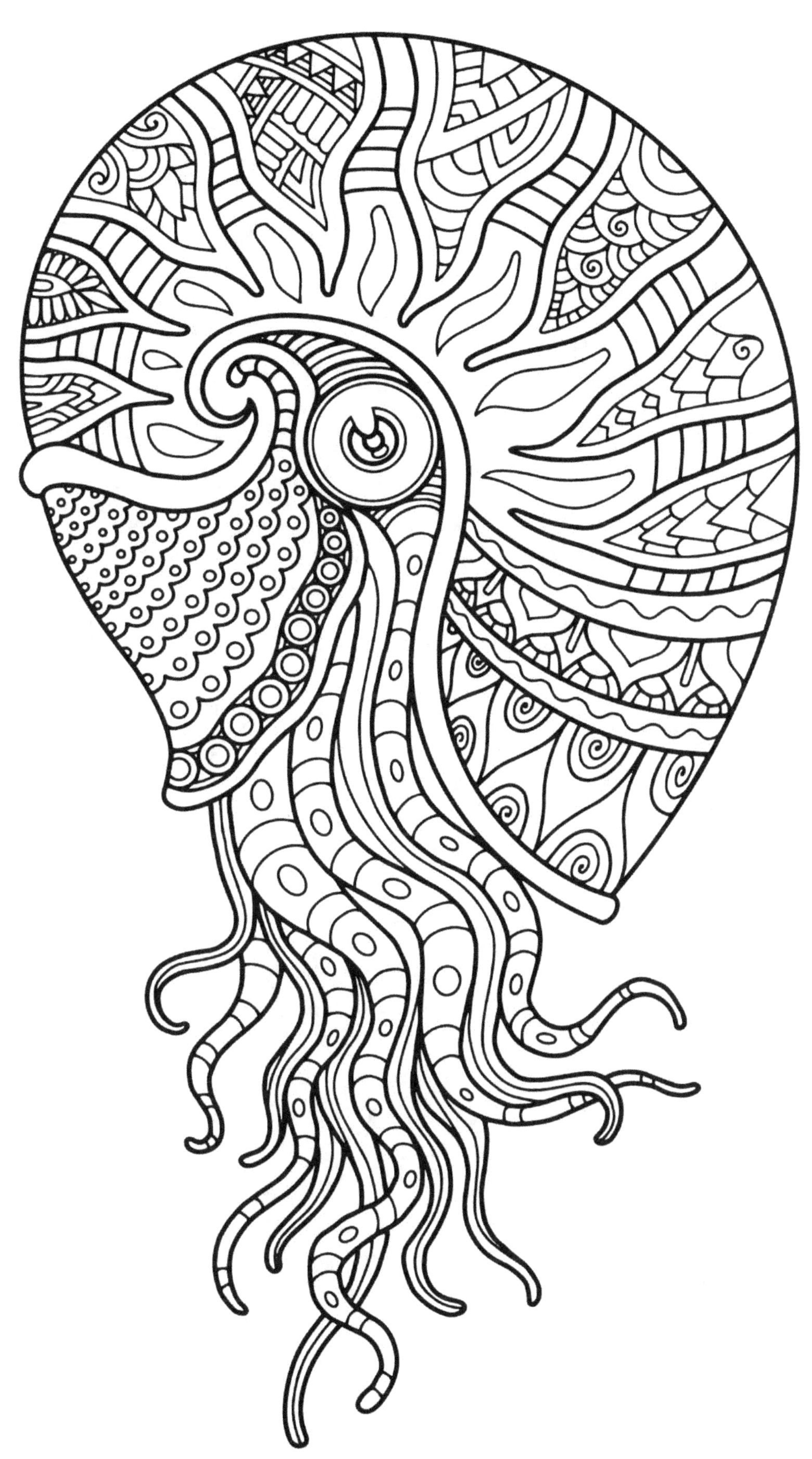

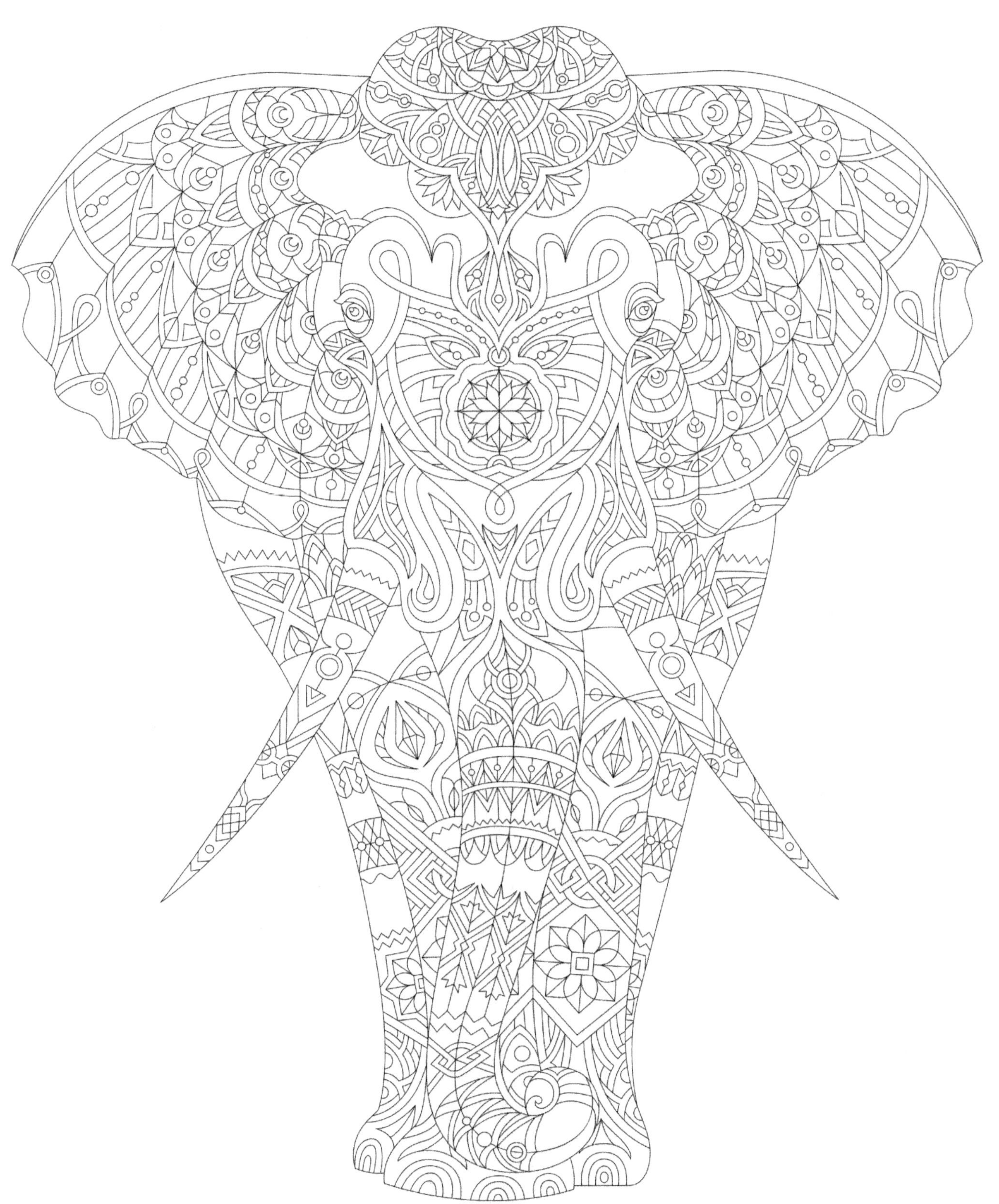

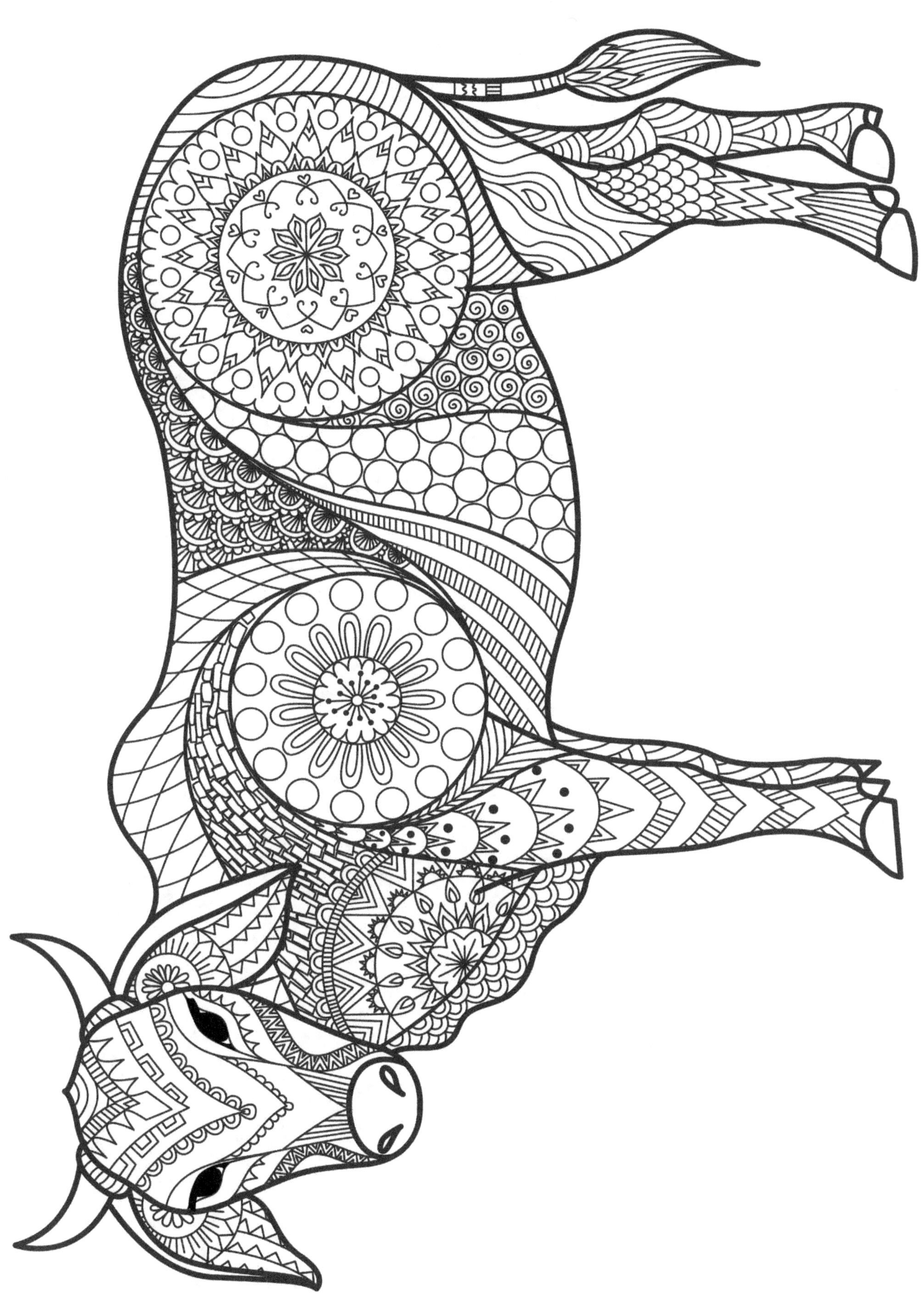

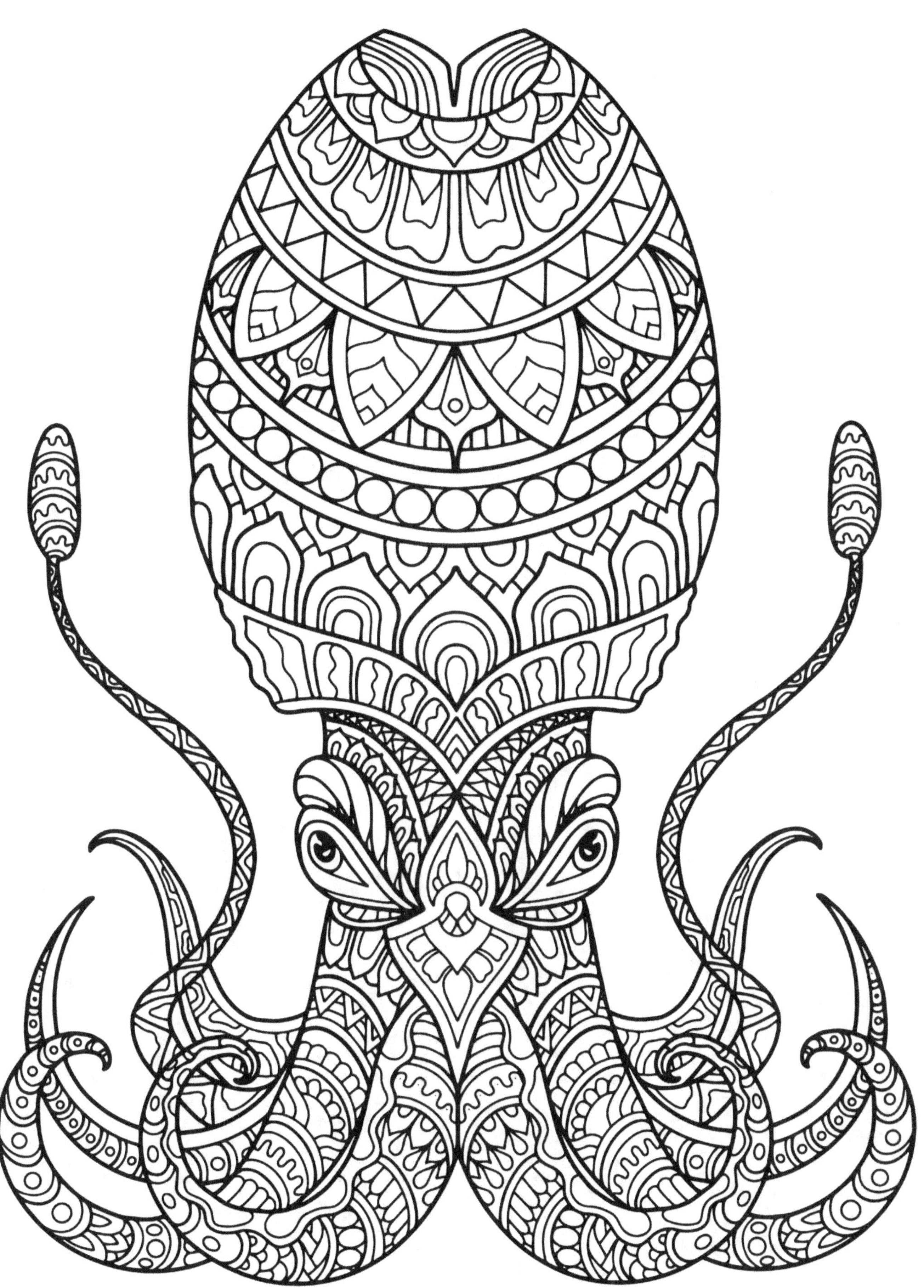

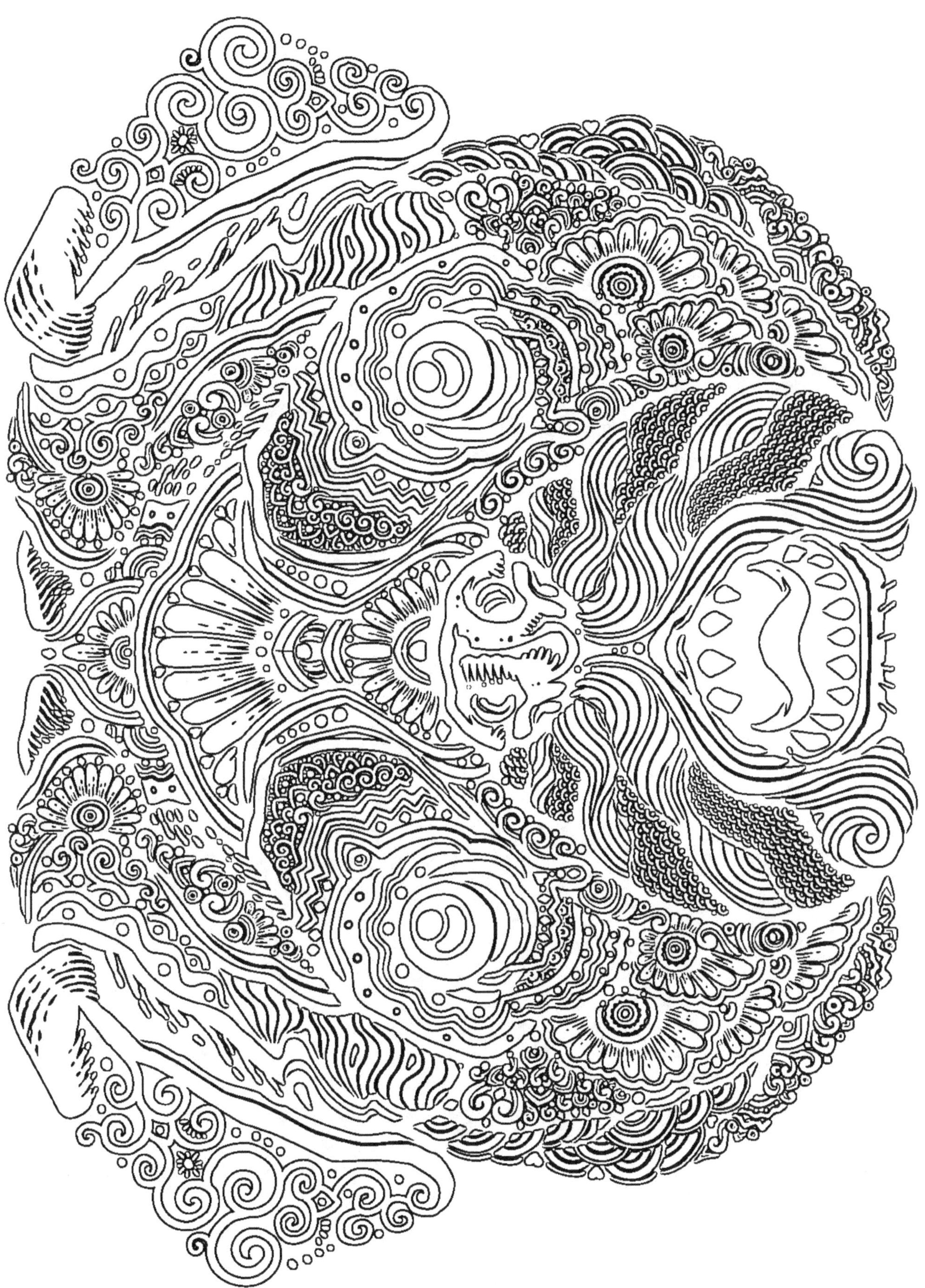

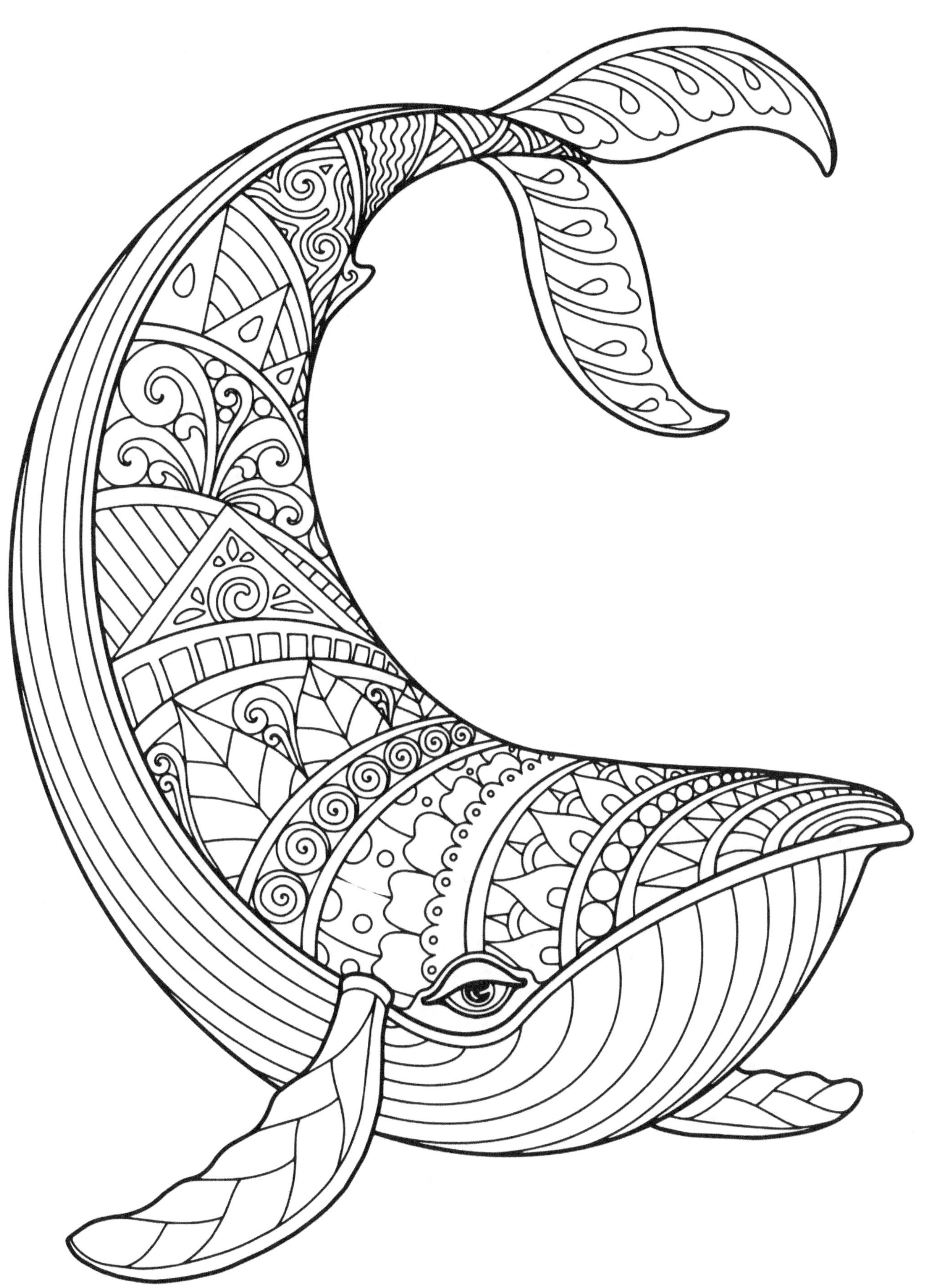

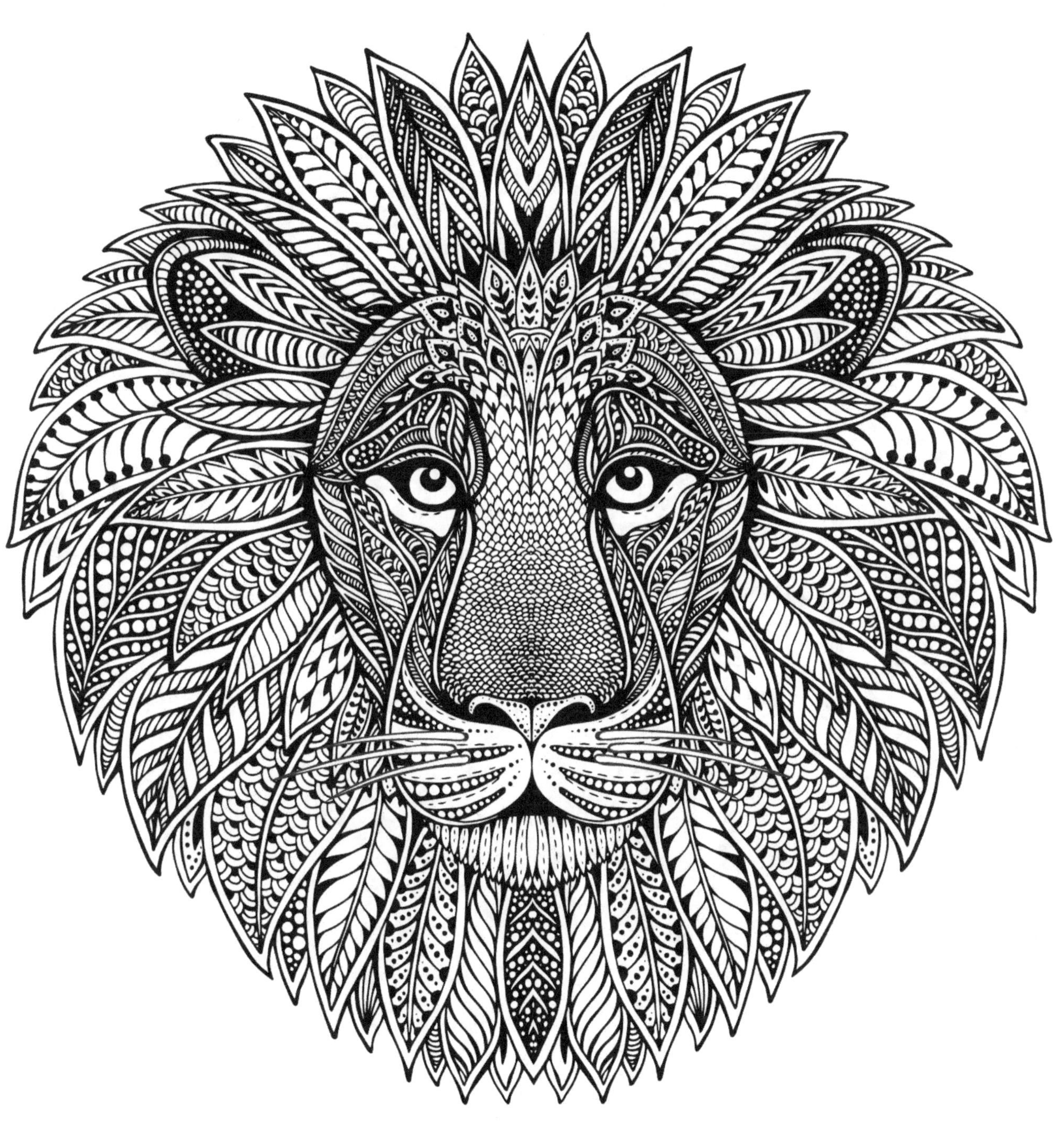

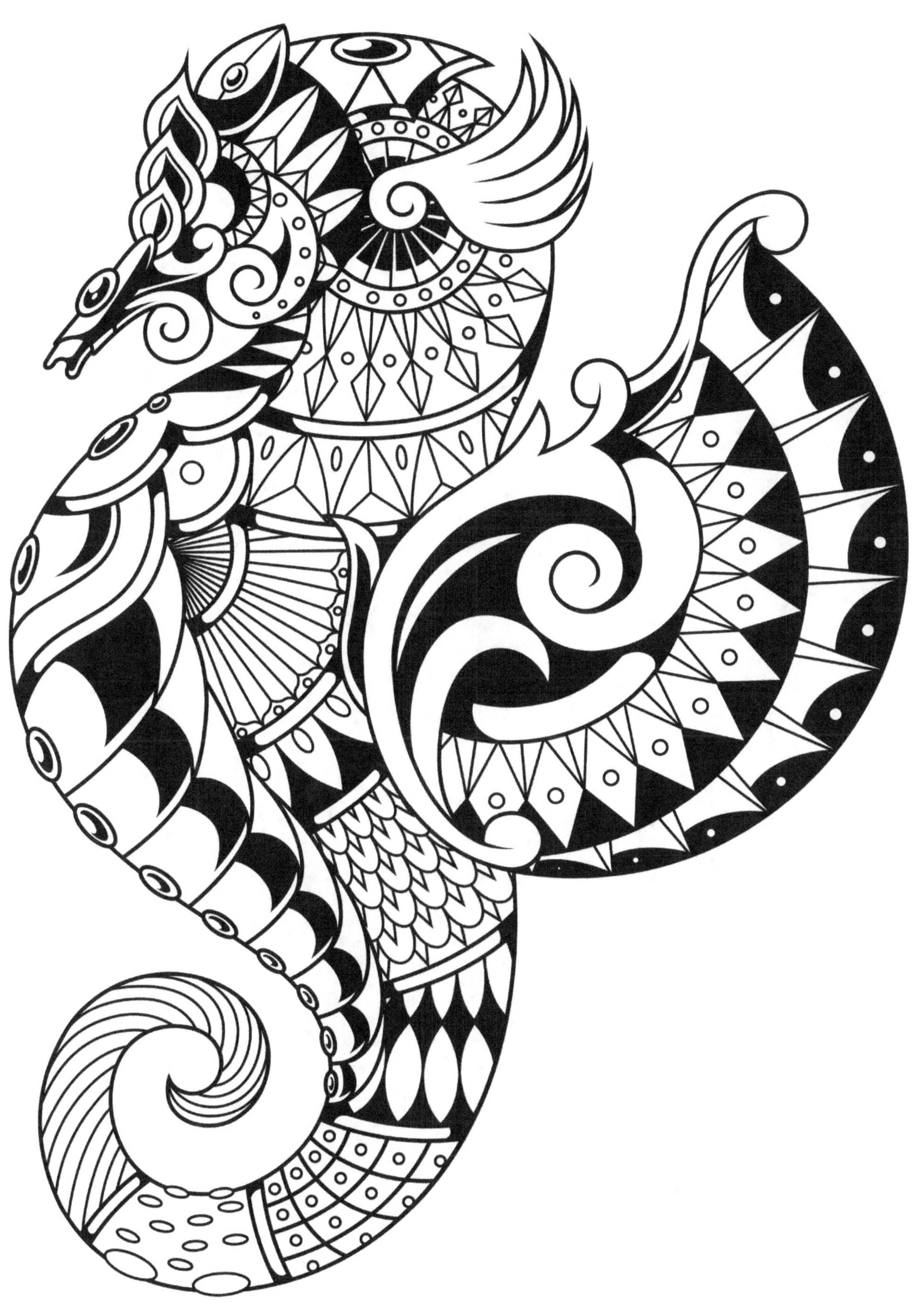

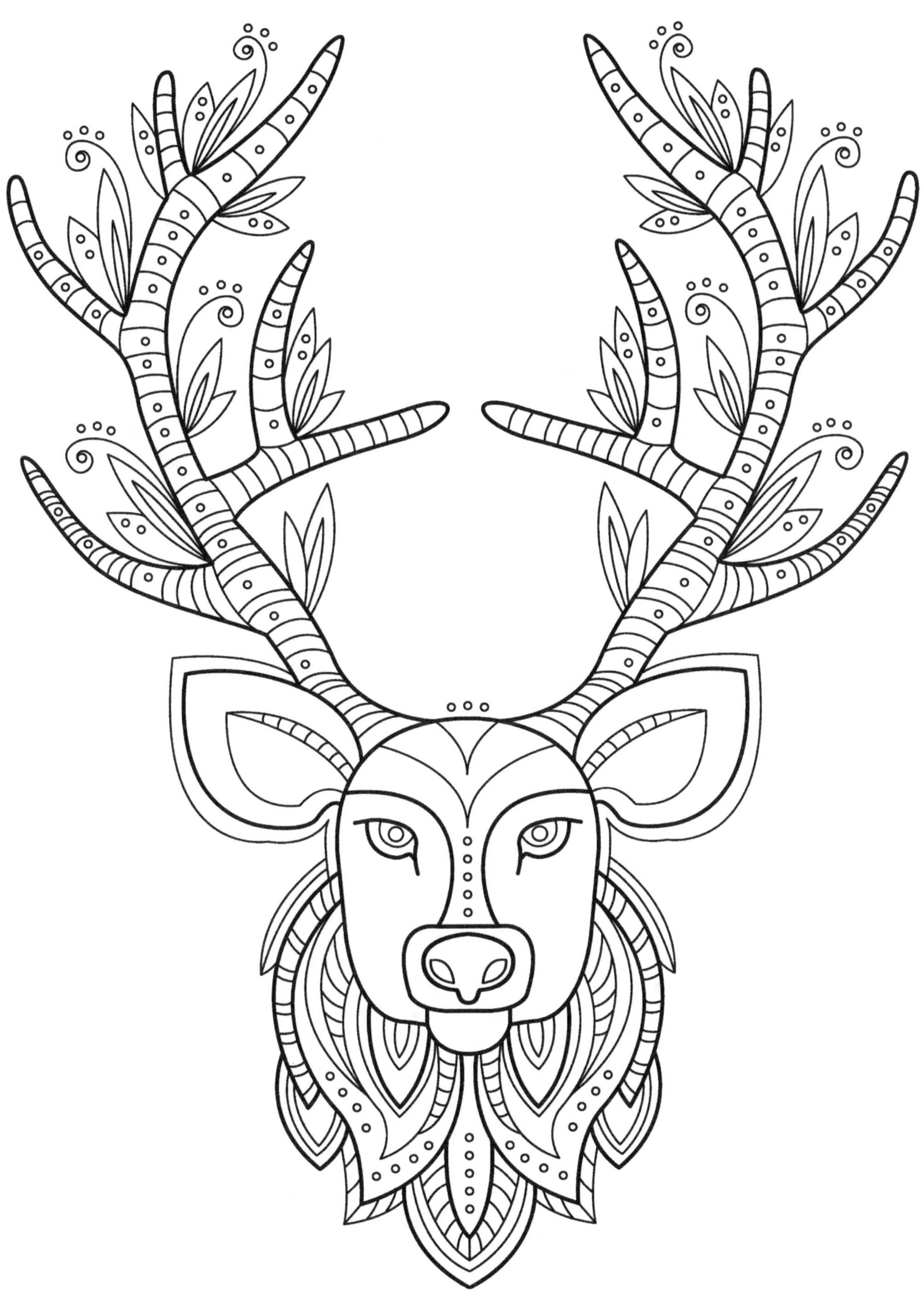

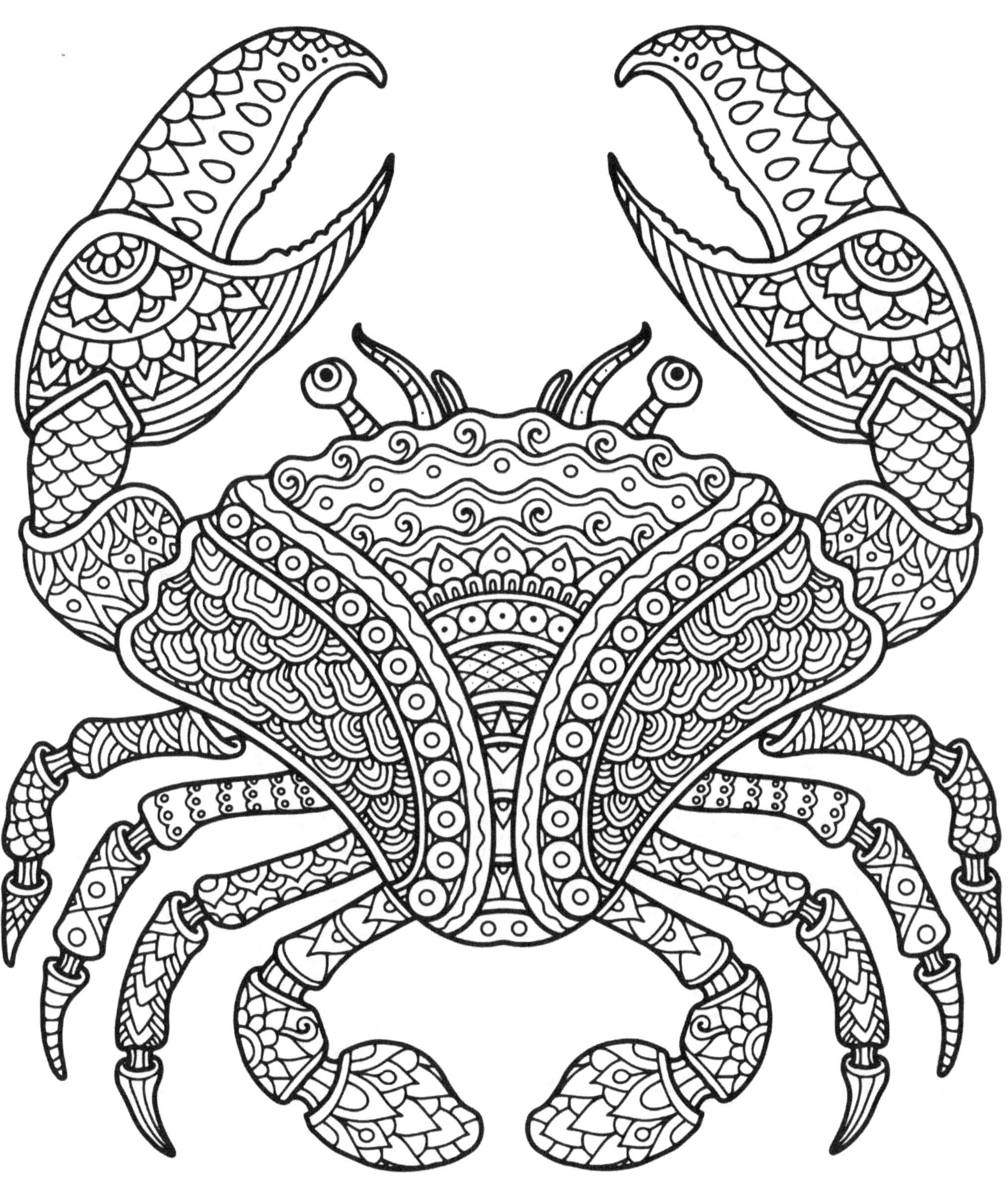

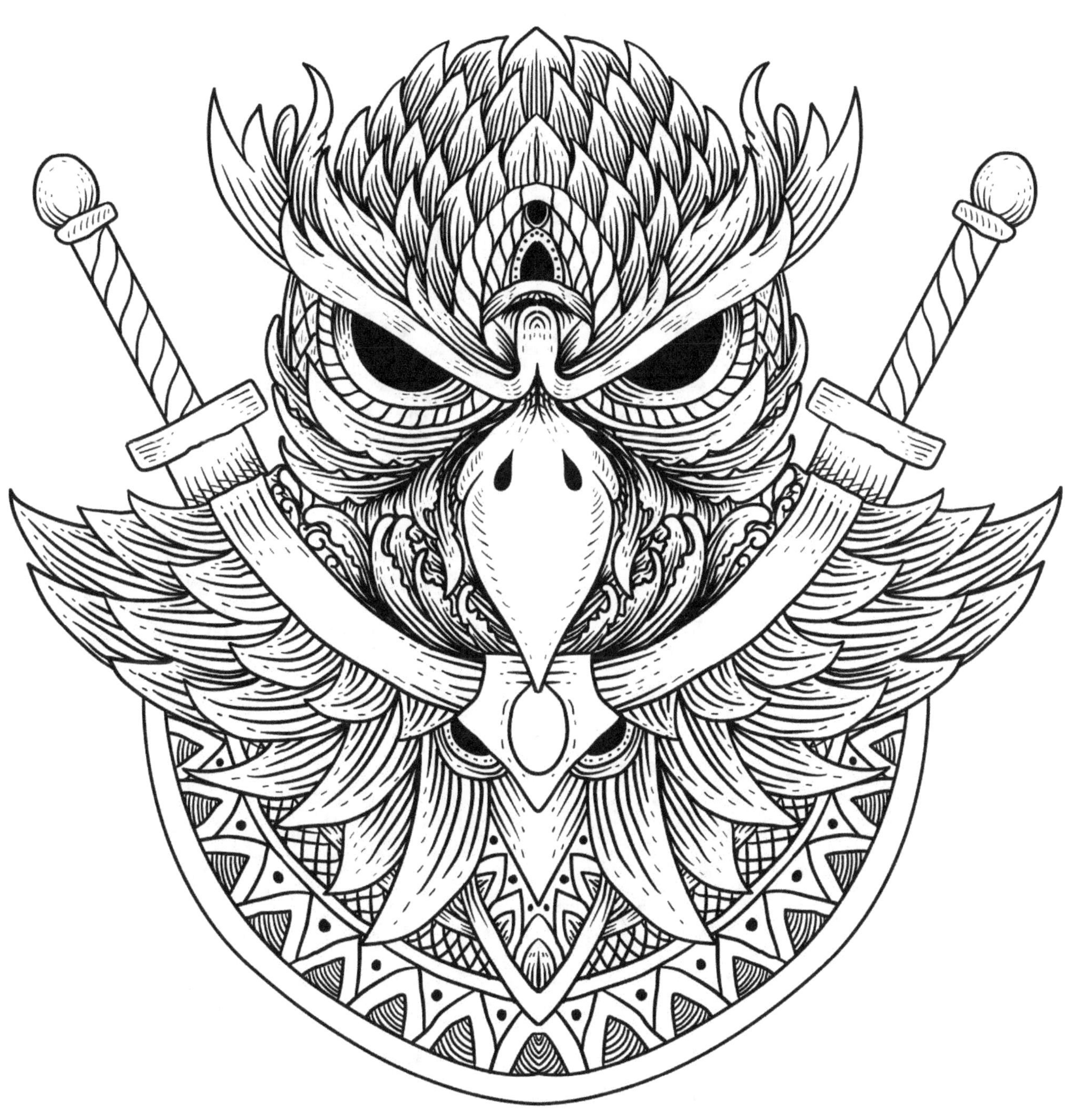

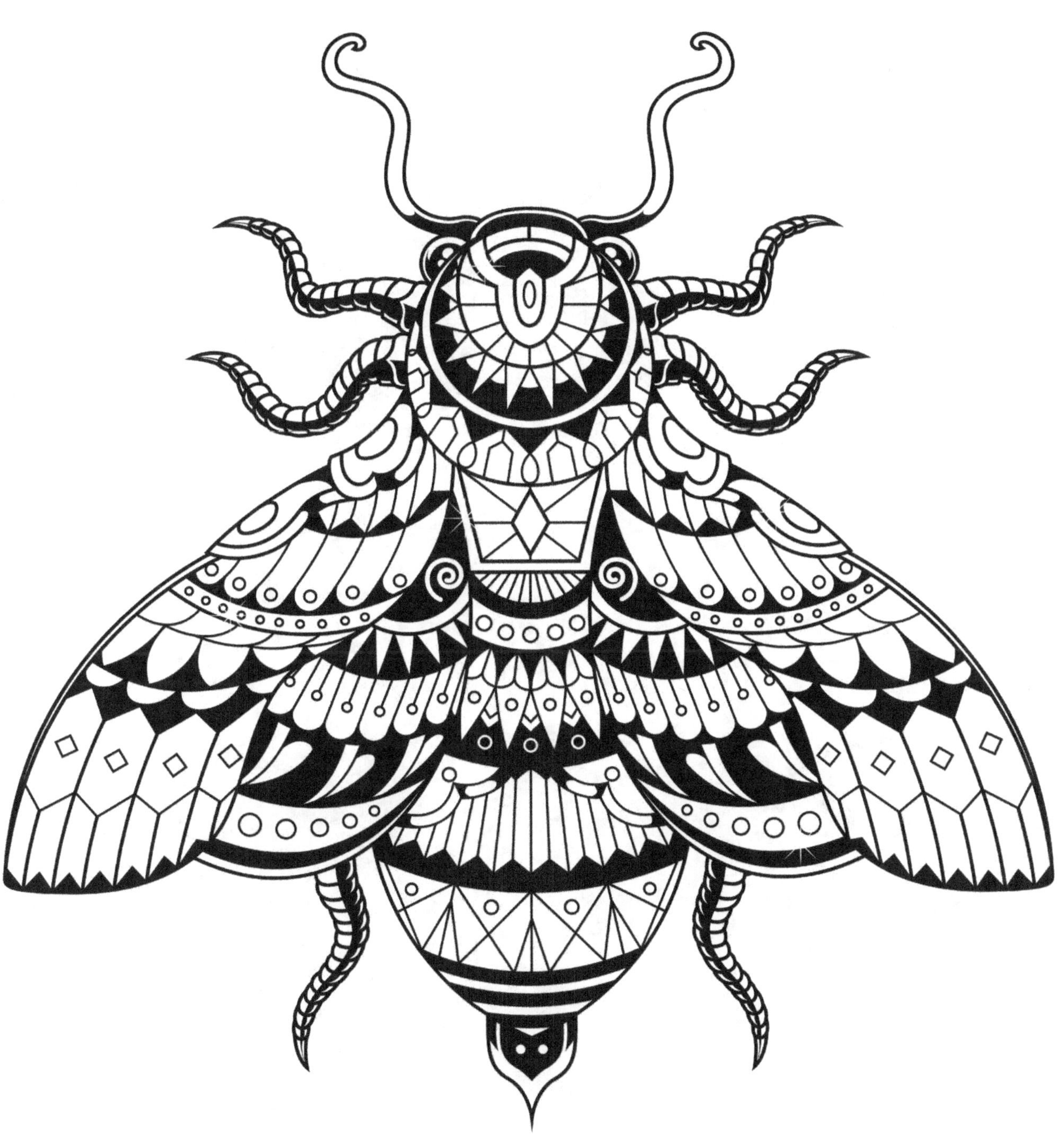

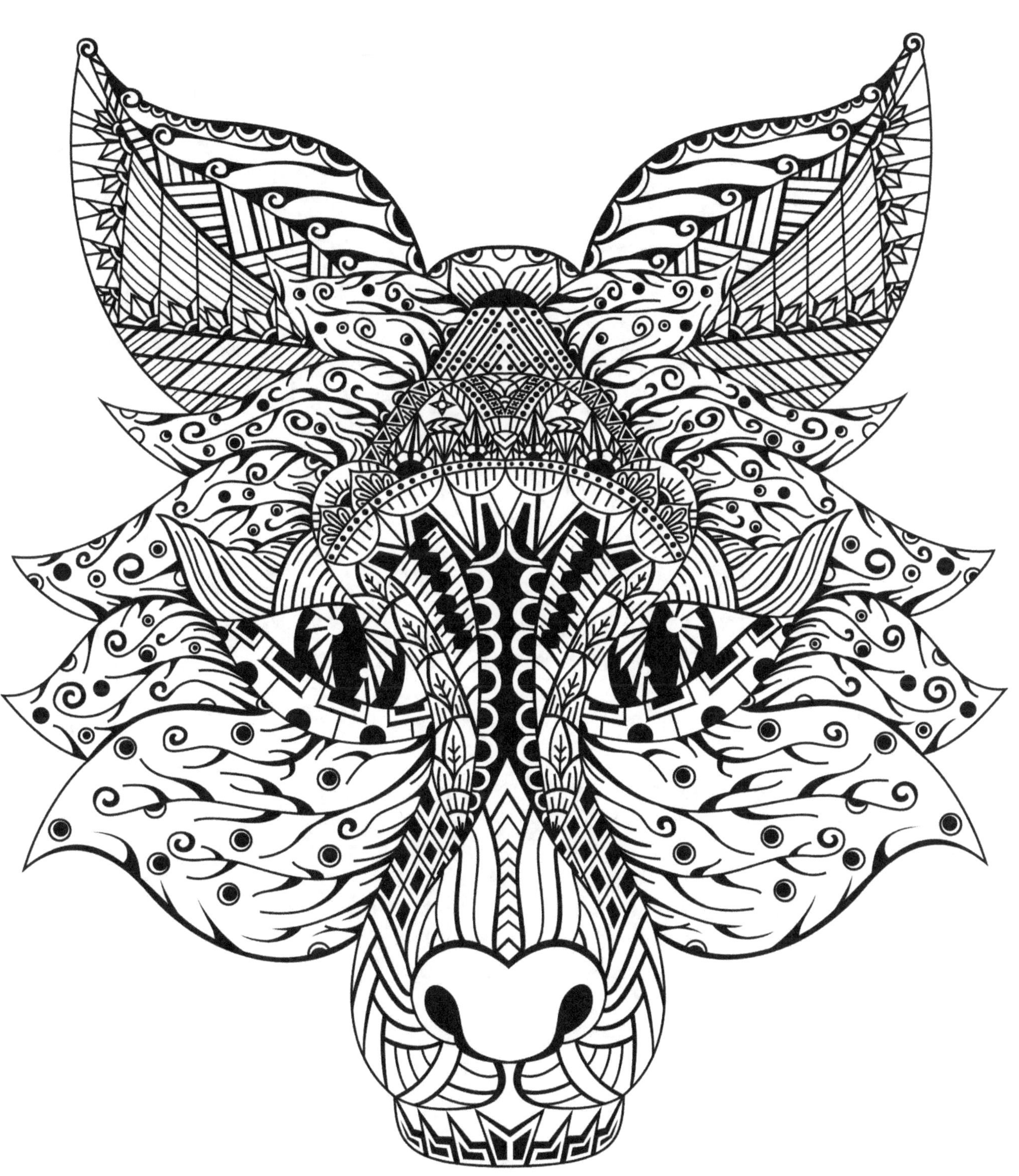

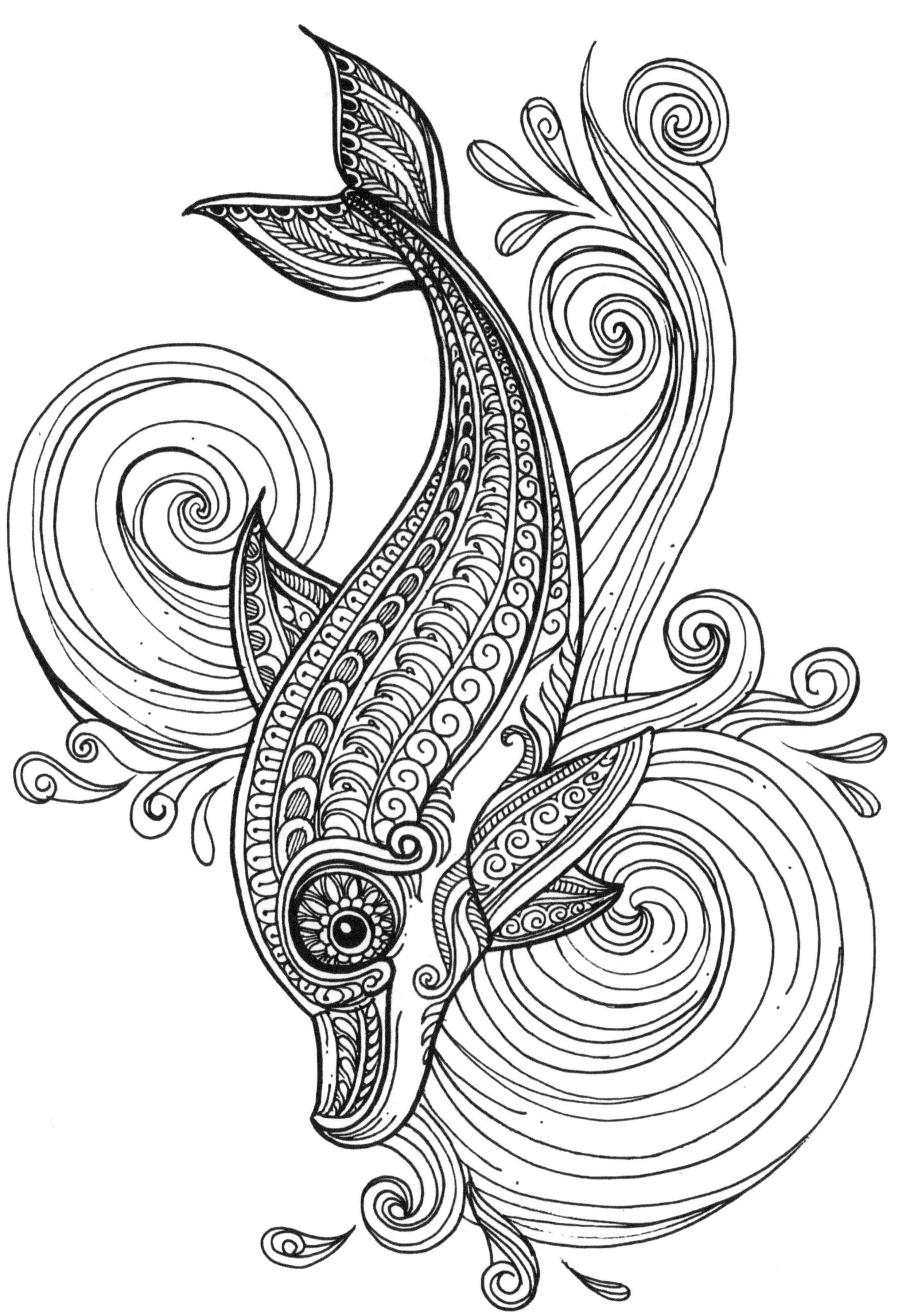

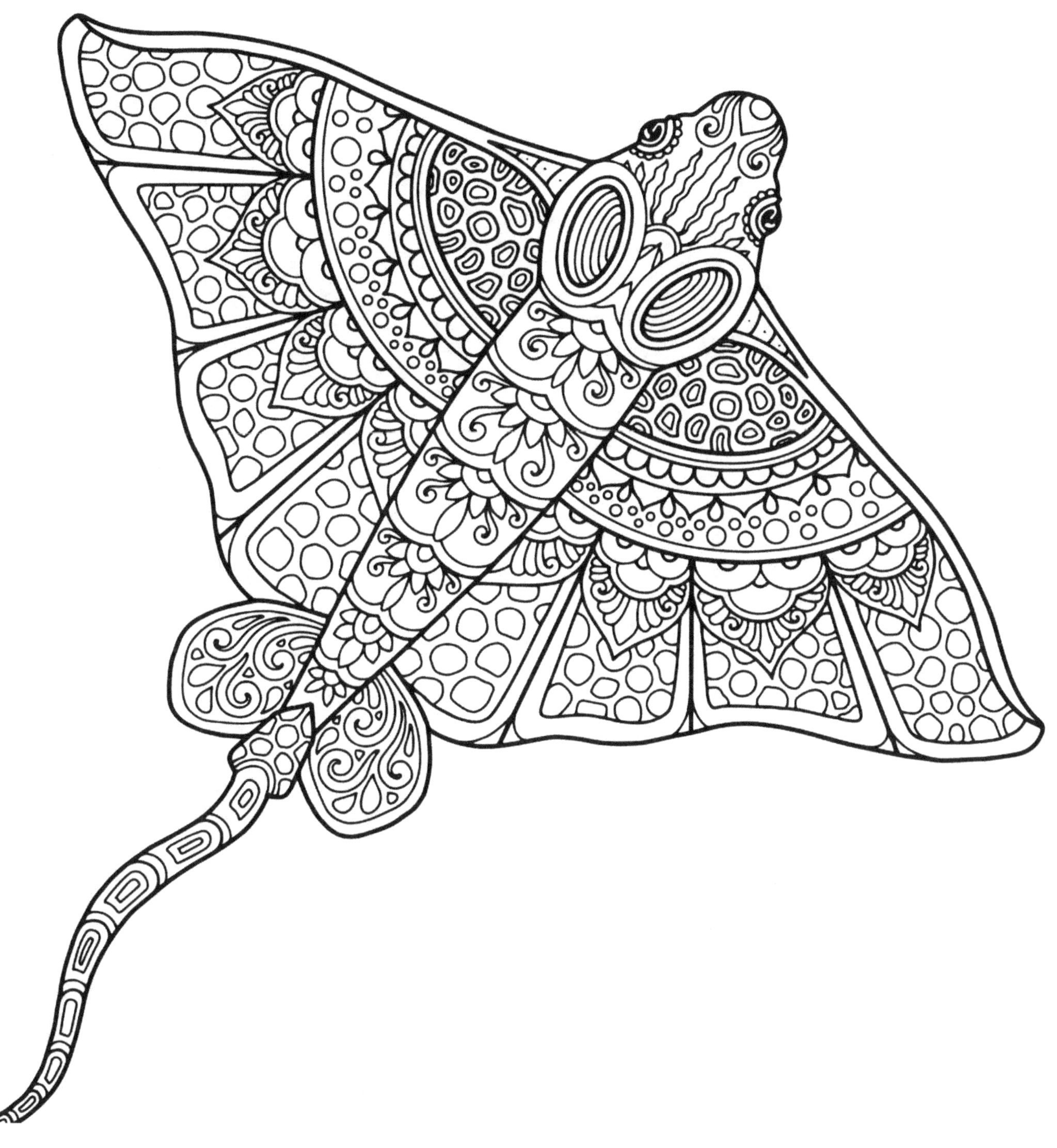

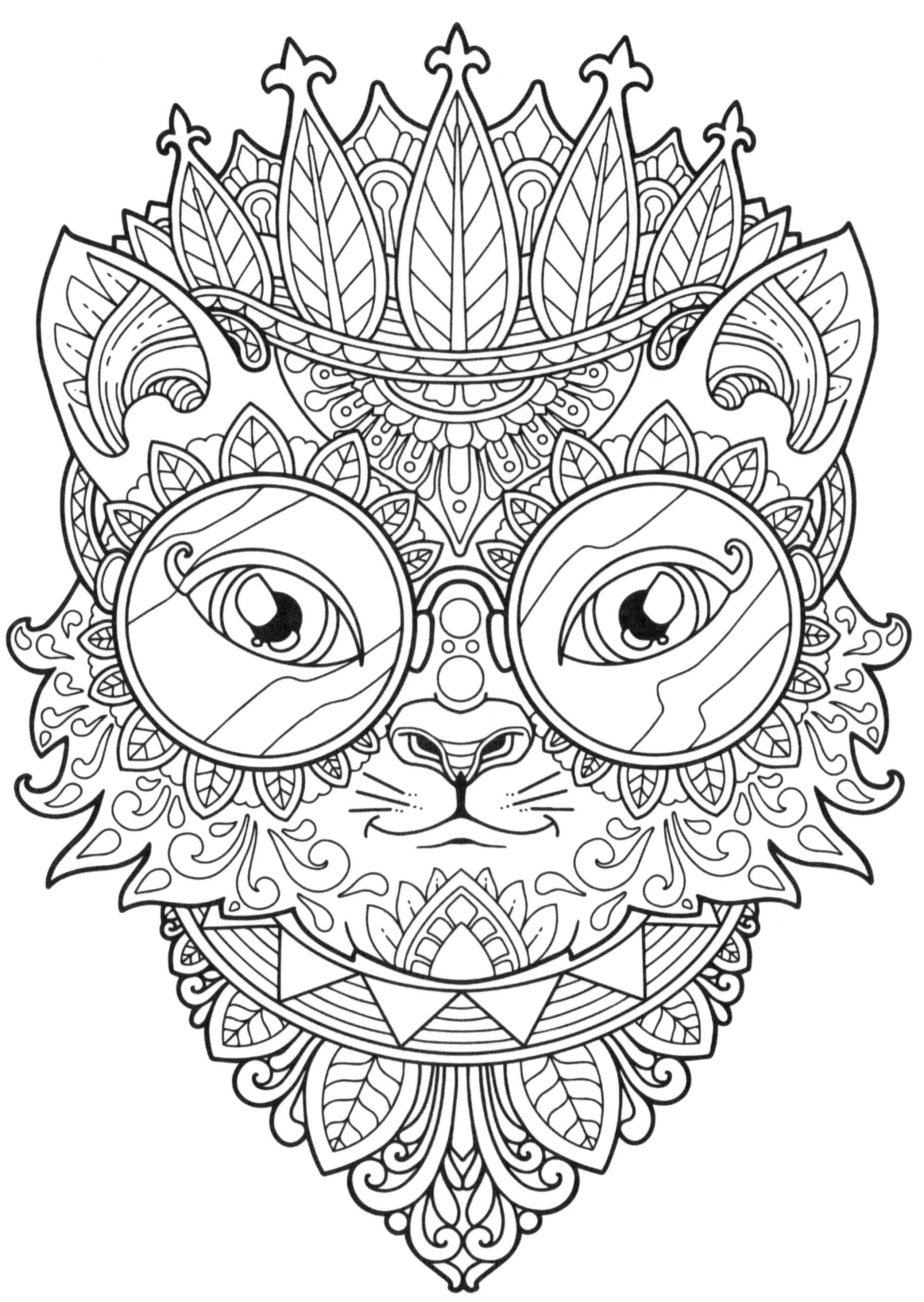

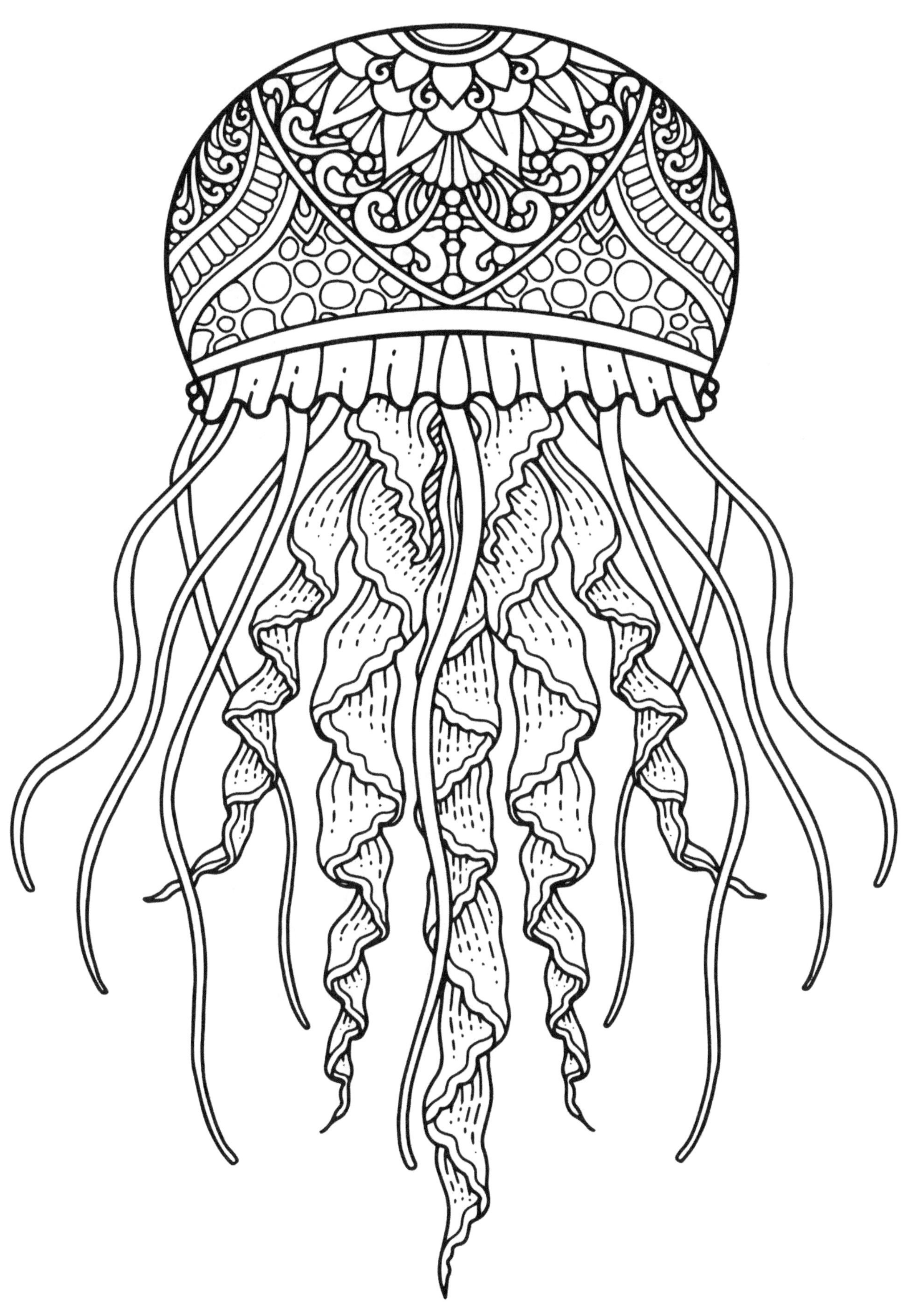

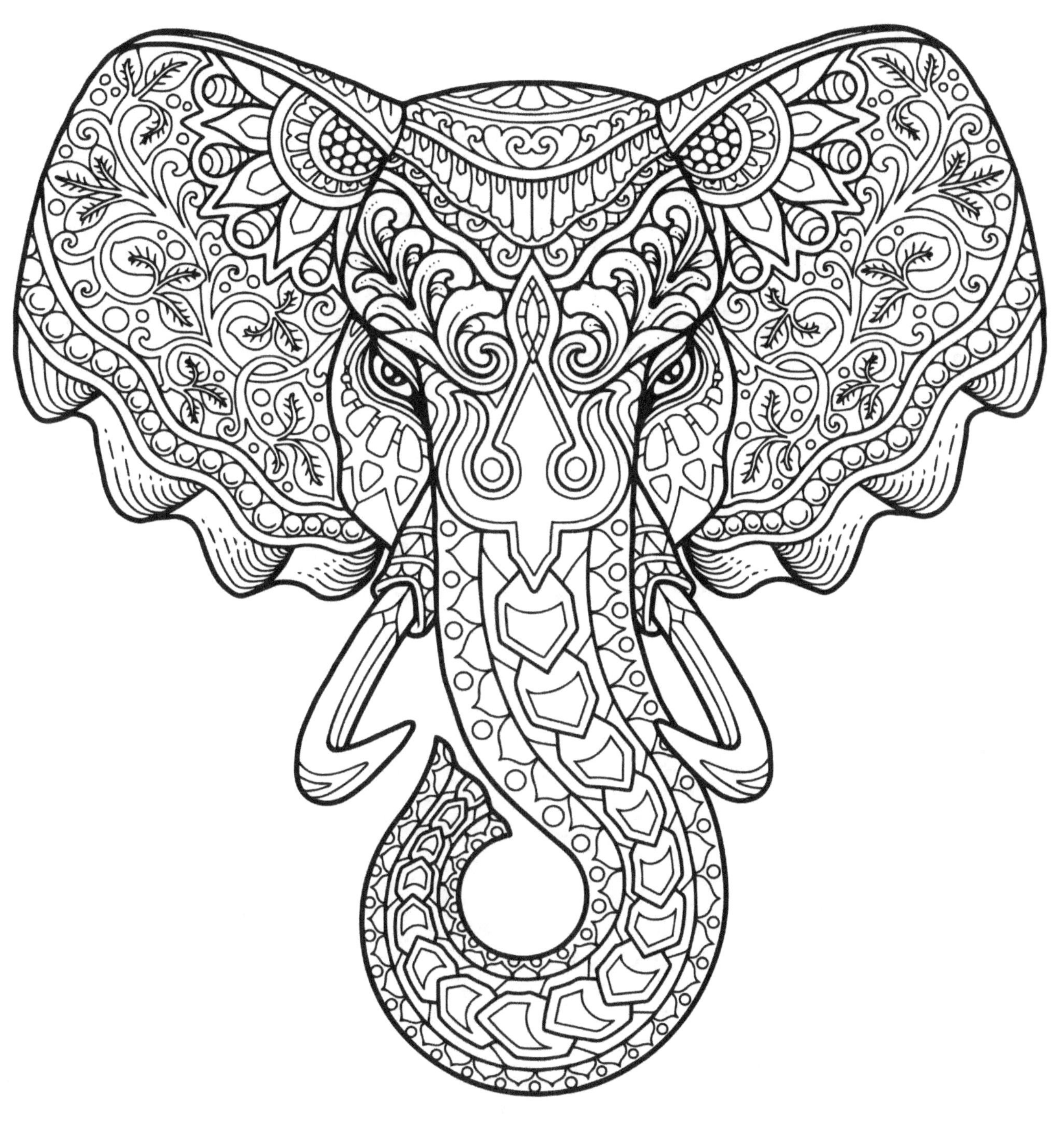

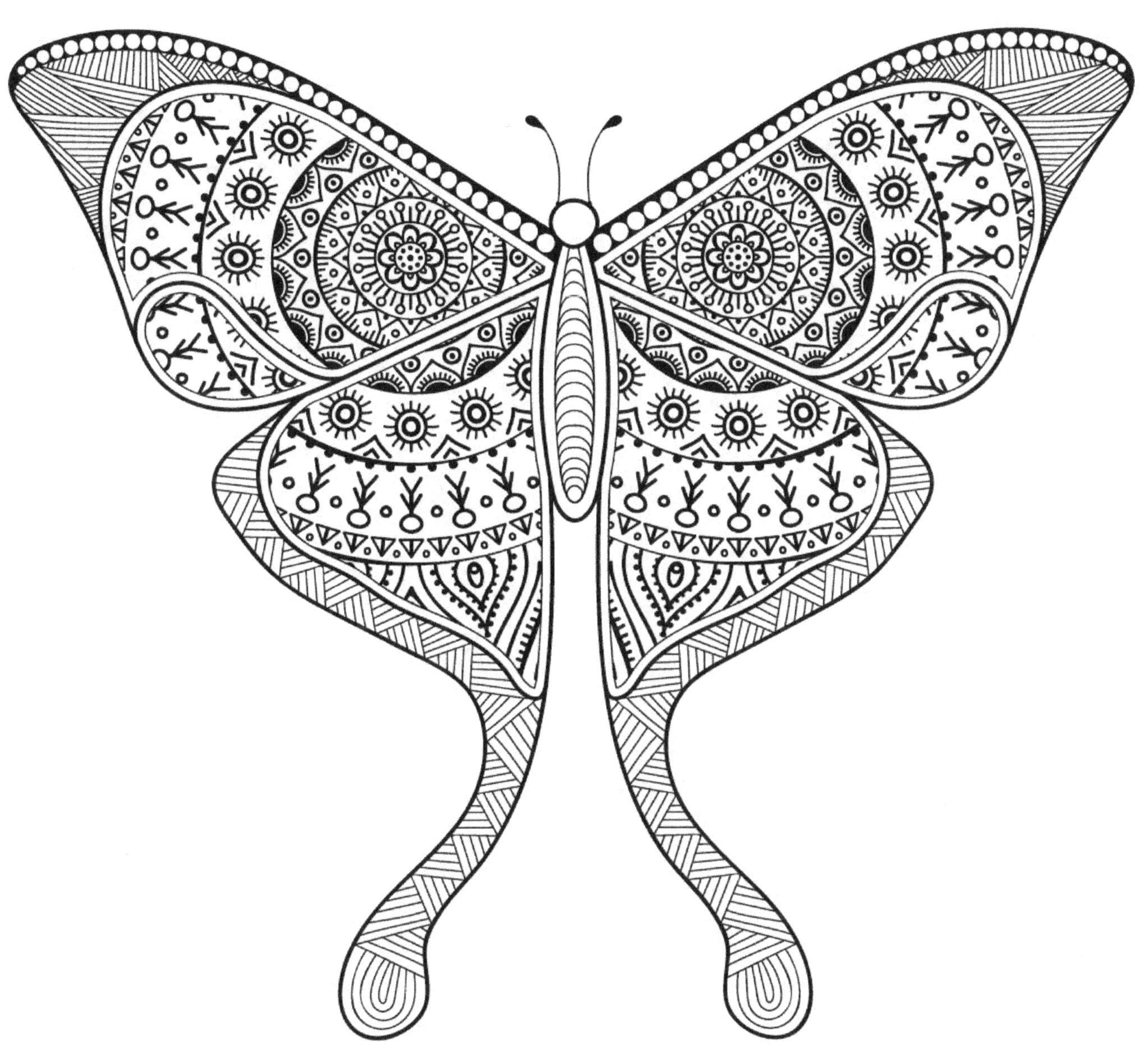

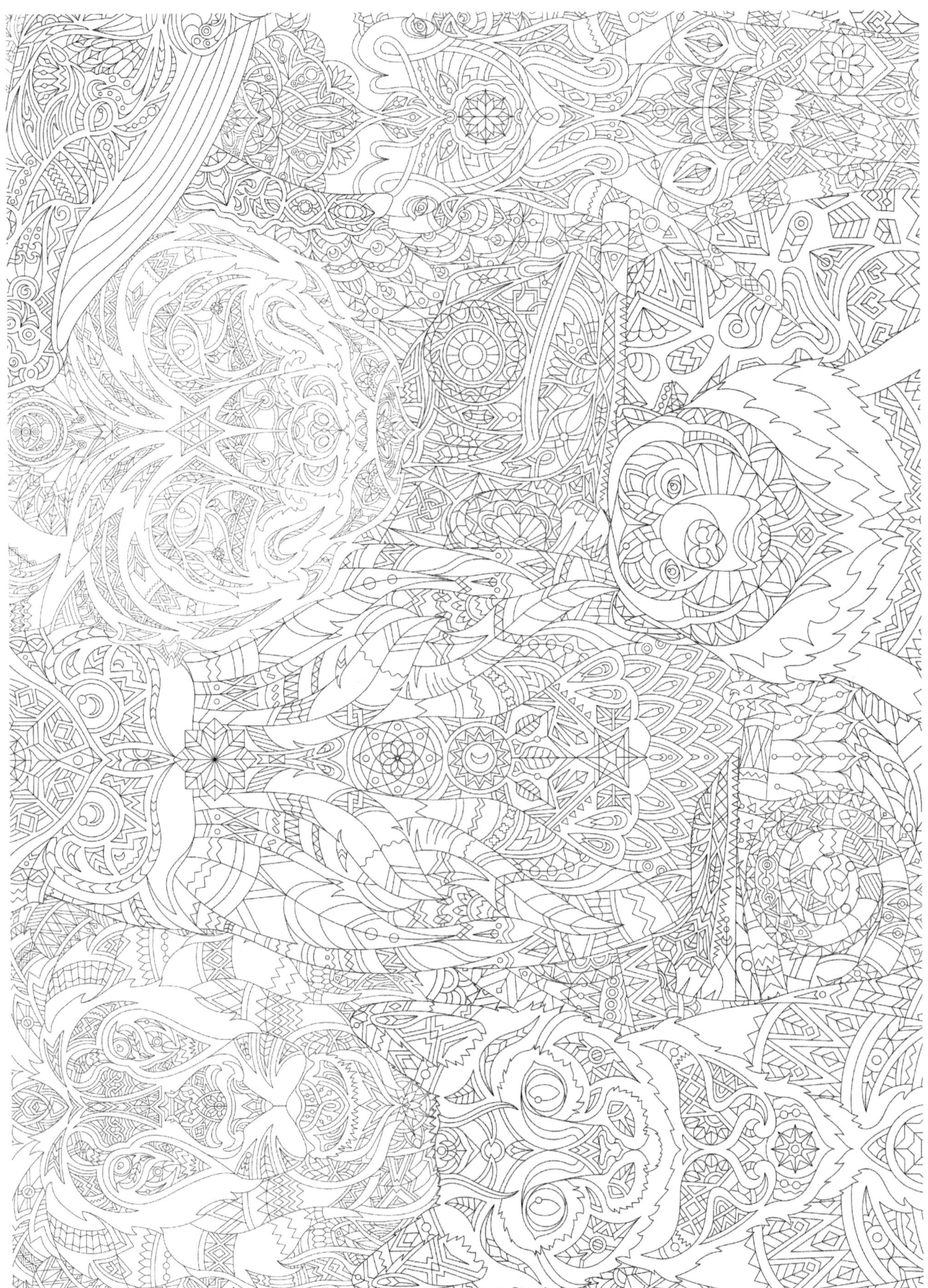

Thank you

We hope you enjoyed our book.

As a small family company, your feedback is important to us.

Please let us know how you like our book at:

golden.books101@gmail.com